ML Answers The 101 Most-Asked Questions

The Lent, Triduum, And Easter Answer Book

Paul J. Niemann

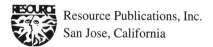
Resource Publications, Inc.
San Jose, California

Reprint Department
Resource Publications, Inc.
160 E. Virginia Street #290
San Jose, CA 95112-5876
(408) 286-8505 voice
(408) 287-8748 fax

Library of Congress Cataloging-in-Publication Data
Niemann, Paul J., 1954–
    The Lent, Triduum, and Easter answer book / Paul Niemann.
       p.   cm. — (ML answers the 101 most-asked questions)
    Includes bibliographical references and index.
    ISBN 0-89390-447-3
      1. Lent — Miscellanea.   2. Paschal triduum — Miscellanea.
    3. Easter — Miscellanea.   4. Catholic Church — Doctrines — Miscellanea.
    I. Title.   II. Series.
    BV85.N49   1998
    263'.92—dc21

Printed in the United States of America
98 99 00 01 02 | 5 4 3 2 1

Contents

Preface: Why Another Book on Lent, Triduum, and Easter? vii

Groundwork Questions
  1. What is included in the seasons of Lent and Easter? 3
  2. How are the forty days of Lent counted? 4
  3. What is the Triduum? 6
  4. What is the Easter season? 7
  5. How is the date of Easter determined?
     Why do Orthodox Christians have a different date? 8

Lent
  6. Why do we wear ashes on Ash Wednesday when the Gospel
     advises us to make no outward display of religion? 13
  7. What is the significance of forty days? 14
  8. What is fasting? 15
  9. What is abstinence? 16
 10. What is the origin of Mardi Gras or Carnival? 17
 11. How are the main themes of Lent presented in the lectionary? . . 18
 12. What are the liturgical symbols of Lent? 21
 13. Is there a rite for "burying the alleluia"? 22
 14. What is the meaning of veiling statues and images during Lent? . 23
 15. What about the use of holy water during Lent?
     Should the font be empty? 24
 16. What kind of decorations are appropriate for Lent? 25

17. We used to conclude stations of the cross with benediction.
    Is this no longer appropriate? 26
18. Are weddings permitted during Lent? 28
19. May infants be baptized during Lent? 29
20. What are our options for penance services? 30
21. How are saints' days celebrated during Lent? 32
22. Is the Liturgy of the Hours different during Lent? 33
23. What is Laetare Sunday? 35
24. What is Passiontide? 36
25. What is Holy Week? 37
26. What is the Chrism Mass? 38
27. Why is the feast of the Annunciation (March 25) celebrated
    after Easter some years? 39
28. May a funeral take place during the Triduum? 40
29. What are the proper liturgical colors of these days? 41
30. Are there any restrictions on music during Lent and Triduum? . . 42
31. What aspects of the Rite of Christian Initiation of Adults
    are proper to Lent? 43
32. What is the rite of election? 44
33. Why is the bishop the presiding celebrant of the rite of election? . 46
34. Are candidates also elected? 47
35. Whose names are inscribed in the Book of the Elect? 48
36. What is "purification and enlightenment?" 49
37. What is a scrutiny? What is an exorcism? 50
38. Do the candidates also participate in the scrutinies? 52
39. What are the presentations? 53
40. What is the meaning of the oil of catechumens? 54

Triduum

41. When does the Triduum begin? 57
42. What is meant by "Maundy Thursday?" 58
43. What are the main elements of the Mass of the Lord's Supper? . . 59
44. What is the significance of the mandatum or footwashing? 61
45. Who may participate in the mandatum rite? 62
46. How are the holy oils used during this Mass? 63
47. Our parish priests renewed their ordination vows at this Mass
    last year. Is this something new? 64

48. What is meant by the paschal fast? How is the paschal fast
distinct from the lenten fast? 65
49. May communion be given during the Triduum apart from Mass
or liturgical services? 66
50. Should Christians celebrate Passover? 67
51. What is the Easter duty? 70
52. How is the Eucharist reserved during the Triduum? 71
53. How does adoration of the Eucharist take place? 72
54. What is meant by "Tenebrae"? 73
55. Is it advisable to have the stations of the cross on Good Friday? . 75
56. What is the current thinking on proclaiming the Passion "in parts?" 76
57. Must there be a homily on Good Friday? 77
58. Should we use a cross or a crucifix for the veneration of the cross? 78
59. Why is there no sign of peace during the Good Friday liturgy? . . 80
60. Why is communion only under the form of bread on Good Friday? 81
61. What do we do with the Blessed Sacrament after the
Good Friday liturgy? 82
62. Where is the cross placed after the Good Friday liturgy? 83
63. Our pastor says that it is now forbidden to hear confessions
on Holy Saturday. Why is this so? 84
64. Why is there Evening Prayer on Holy Saturday but not on
Holy Thursday and Good Friday? 85
65. How early may the Easter Vigil begin? 86
66. Any suggestions for the Easter fire? 87
67. Must we buy a new paschal candle every year? 88
68. How many readings must be used for the Vigil? 89
69. May we use other songs in place of the responsorial psalm? . . . 91
70. How is the alleluia to be sung at the Vigil? 92
71. What do the Elect do on Holy Saturday? 93
72. What about those who are not being baptized this year? 94
73. We have never baptized anyone by immersion before.
How can we introduce this option? 95
74. How do we baptize some, receive others, and renew
the baptismal promises of everyone in the same service?
When should the sprinkling rite take place? 97
75. Should the candidates wear baptismal robes? 98
76. Isn't confirmation only administered by the bishop? 99
77. After all the other ceremonies of the Vigil, the prayer
of the faithful seems redundant. Can it be omitted? 100

78. We would like to make the catechumens' first communion
    more special. What can we do? 101
79. The neighboring parish had a blessing of food after the
    Easter Vigil. What is the significance of that custom? 102
80. When should we decorate the church for Easter? 103

Easter

81. What are the liturgical symbols of Easter? 107
82. How is the Easter season presented in the lectionary? 109
83. What is the purpose of the Sequence on Easter Sunday morning? 110
84. Should we renew baptismal promises again on Easter Sunday? . . 111
85. What is the octave of Easter? 112
86. What about funerals and weddings during the octave of Easter? . 113
87. Our parish never uses the sprinkling rite except during
    Easter time. Why is this? 114
88. The fifty days of Easter just seem lost among all the other
    activities. How can we emphasize them? 115
89. How are the saints commemorated during the Easter season? . . . 116
90. What were the Rogation Days and Ember Days? 117
91. Why does our music director refuse to play hymns to the
    Blessed Mother during May? 118
92. What is the May Crowning devotion? 120
93. What's wrong with preaching about Mother's Day? 122
94. What ever happened to Ascension Thursday? 124
95. Isn't the Easter candle supposed to be put away
    after the Ascension? 125
96. I heard of a parish that has a novena to the Holy Spirit.
    What is that? 126
97. How can we celebrate the Vigil of Pentecost? 127
98. Shouldn't we renew our confirmation on Pentecost, just like we
    renewed our baptism at Easter? 128
99. Why do some people call Pentecost "the birthday of the church"? 129
100. Should other languages be used for the Pentecost Sequence? . . . 130
101. I understand that the Easter season concludes with Pentecost.
     How can we symbolize that? 131

Works Cited and Suggested 133
Index 135

Preface: Why Another Book on Lent, Triduum, and Easter?

The paschal mystery of the death, burial, and resurrection of Jesus Christ is the heart of the Christian faith. The paschal mystery is celebrated every Sunday, the Lord's Day, as well as in every Eucharist; indeed, the entire liturgical life of the church draws us into the redemptive work of Christ. The "ninety days" of Lent, Triduum, and Easter, the liturgical celebration of this paschal mystery, comprise a unique moment of grace in the liturgical year.

The purpose of this book is to help the reader more deeply appreciate the paschal mystery itself and the unique way in which it is celebrated in the Roman Catholic liturgical tradition. Although it is designed for parish ministers, especially for those just beginning to work with parish liturgy, it will be of interest to all who seek to deepen their understanding of the liturgy. The questions and answers which follow are offered as a resource to those who plan liturgical celebrations in the Roman Catholic tradition. They may also serve as a point of reflection and evaluation for those whose celebrations would benefit from taking a closer look at why we do what we do as a church at worship.

The enduring genius of the Roman liturgy is its simplicity; it serves as a pattern or ground-plan which has been adapted and used by many people through the centuries. If you want to be a competent liturgy planner, you should have a deep respect for that basic order of worship. In musical terms, you need to know the scales and keys before you can improvise. In artistic terms, you must know the basics of color, form, and composition before you develop your own style. There is no substitute for mastery of the principles of ritual worship.

Those who prepare liturgical celebrations should be familiar with the sacramentary, the lectionary, the *Rite of Christian Initiation of Adults*, the *Liturgy of the Hours*, the *Book of Blessings*, and the introductions contained within each of these resources. Instructions such as *General Norms for the Liturgical Year and the Calendar*, the *Ceremonial of Bishops*, and the *Circular Letter for the Preparation and Celebration of the Easter Feasts* are also essential resources. Being "familiar" does not mean memorizing the contents, nor does it imply that the answer to every pastoral or ritual question is found within them. These resources preserve our common heritage and our liturgical principles.

The Roman Catholic Church, like any other human society or organization, has a system of laws to help support its community life and mission. Usually "church law" refers to "canon law." However, the *Code of Canon Law* is not designed to regulate the celebration of the liturgy. Canon 2 notes that "the Code does not define the rites which are to be observed in celebrating liturgical actions. For this reason current liturgical norms retain their force...." The liturgical documents and instructions named above are another (and just as important) part of church law.[1]

While this seems simple enough, there are thousands of pages of documents concerning the liturgy.[2] Each document carries a particular authority. Some documents, such as the *General Instruction of the Roman Missal*, are promulgated by the pope and affect the universal church. These general instructions leave some matters to the decision of the national bishops' conference or the local diocesan bishop, others to the pastor of the parish, still others to the presider at a particular celebration. To assure the proper understanding and implementation

---

1 Descriptions of the liturgy or the sacraments in sources such as the *Catechism of the Catholic Church* are exactly that: descriptions. These, too, are not the norms to be observed in the actual celebration but are designed to help teach the meaning of the rites.

2 Most of the documents which apply to parish celebrations are located in the front of the liturgical books themselves. For example, the *General Instruction of the Roman Missal* is in the sacramentary. Another useful source is *The Liturgy Documents* (see "Works Cited and Suggested").

of the rites, other instructions, such as the *Circular Letter*, are issued by the Vatican Congregation for Divine Worship and Discipline of the Sacraments. These instructions are also meant for the universal church. Further, the bishops' conference, the Bishops' Committee on the Liturgy, the diocesan bishop, or the diocesan office of worship or liturgical commission may issue policies or recommendations in response to national or local pastoral needs. Your diocesan office of worship can help you resolve liturgical questions which may arise after reading the published directives.

Ritual has great power to touch the human spirit. While essentially traditional, that is, handed down to us from those who have gone before, ritual is always done by living people. The liturgy frequently speaks of "today." This is the day, the hour, of the Lord.

Two dangerous tendencies in liturgical worship must be carefully avoided. I say "dangerous" because they drain the life out of liturgy and eventually destroy the spiritual life, the soul, of the worshipers. These two tendencies are *formalism* and *trivialization*. Formalism is the repetition of gesture and word without engagement of mind, heart, and soul. We may carry out the rites in perfect accord with the rubrics, but we have not worshiped. The opposite tendency, trivialization, is a simple appeal to emotions by use of gimmicks. Sometimes "good liturgy" is evaluated on the basis of how we feel immediately after a particular celebration. We may have perhaps made the mystery too comfortable, too casual. We have attempted to domesticate the Holy One, making for ourselves a god in our own image. This is junk food for the soul.

Good liturgical worship provides the people of God with bread from heaven: fresh, tasty, *and* nourishing, made from the old family recipe. It is this living bread which we need in order to bring life to our physically and spiritually hungry world. Only when the world's hungers have been fed can we be assured of the adequacy of our liturgy.

The questions which follow are those that have been asked by clergy, liturgy commission members, religious educators, and others who serve the church at worship. Some questions are quite basic, some are complex; all may be starting points for other discussions in a variety of directions. I can only hope that the searching and discussion which take place beyond these pages will not become an adventure into rubrical trivia or divisive argument. May our questions and conversations bring all of us into holy wonder; may they open us to the river of life, flowing from the throne of God and the Lamb, through the streets of a new Jerusalem. This is the ultimate purpose of liturgical celebration.

Groundwork Questions

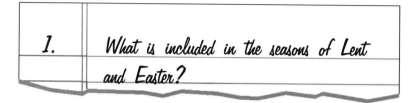

1. *What is included in the seasons of Lent and Easter?*

S ometimes known as the Easter, or paschal, cycle, the seasons of Lent and Easter include all the days from Ash Wednesday through Pentecost Sunday. The three major divisions of this time are:
1. Lent, from Ash Wednesday through Thursday of Holy Week;
2. Triduum, from Holy Thursday evening through Easter Sunday evening;
3. Easter, from Easter Sunday through Pentecost Sunday.

In addition, the days from Palm Sunday until the Triduum are known as *Holy Week*; Easter Sunday through the Second Sunday of Easter is the *Octave of Easter*; and the days between Ascension and Pentecost are often kept as a special time for prayer for the coming of the Holy Spirit.

The weekdays of Lent take precedence over the memorials of the saints; these memorials are then listed simply as "commemorations" and as such are usually celebrated only by those communities which have the saint as a patron or a similar reason for celebration. Two solemnities (St. Joseph, March 19, and Annunciation of the Lord, March 25) and the feast of the Chair of Peter (February 22) are celebrated with their proper liturgies when these occur during Lent.

This represents a simplification from the previous Roman calendar. The former calendar included a period of pre-lenten preparation, marked by Sundays called *Septuagesima, Sexagesima,* and *Quin-quagesima* (representing seventy, sixty, and fifty days until Easter even though these were three consecutive Sundays). This calendar also ended paschal time on the Ascension and added both a vigil and an octave of Pentecost. Because many devotional customs were developed during this older system, parishioners may refer to the Triduum as "the Holy Week services" or may not appreciate the concept of fifty days of Easter.

3

2. How are the forty days of Lent counted?

There are two themes or emphases of the season of Lent: baptism and penance (*Constitution on the Sacred Liturgy* 109).

The lenten season has a double character, namely to prepare both catechumens and faithful to celebrate the Paschal Mystery. The catechumens both with the rite of election and scrutinies, and by catechesis, are prepared for the celebration of the sacraments of Christian initiation; the faithful, ever more attentive to the Word of God and prayer, prepare themselves by penance for the renewal of their baptismal promises (*Circular Letter* 6, quoted in *Ceremonial of Bishops* 249).

The two emphases have provided two enumerations of the "forty days of Lent." In question 11 we will look at the lenten lectionary to see how these themes are presented scripturally.

The "baptismal" or "initiatory" Lent consists of the forty days from the First Sunday of Lent through Thursday of the sixth week of Lent (Holy Week). These forty days are also called the period of purification and enlightenment. This is a special time of prayer for the elect, that is, those preparing for baptism at the Easter Vigil.

Lent is also the principal time of reflection for all the faithful on their own baptism as well as on the mysteries of conversion, repentance, and reconciliation. This penitential or ascetical emphasis is symbolized by the lenten fast. Because Sundays are never days of penance, Lent is also counted as forty days of fasting from Ash Wednesday through Holy Saturday inclusive: six weeks (not including Sundays) plus the four days from Ash Wednesday on.

This dual enumeration leads to some confusion about when Lent begins and ends. Both Ash Wednesday and the First Sunday of Lent have texts and rites which mark the beginning of Lent:

Lord,
protect us in our struggle against evil.
As we begin the discipline of Lent,

make this day holy by our self-denial
(Opening Prayer, Ash Wednesday; emphasis added).

The *first Sunday of Lent marks the beginning of the annual lenten observance.* In the Mass of this Sunday there should be some distinctive elements which underline this important moment, e.g., the entrance procession with litanies of the saints. During the Mass of the first Sunday in Lent, the bishop should celebrate the rite of election in the cathedral or in some other church, as seems appropriate (*Circular Letter* 23; emphasis added).

The official calendar notes that "Lent runs from Ash Wednesday *until the Mass of the Lord's Supper exclusive*" (*General Norms for the Liturgical Year and the Calendar* 28; emphasis added), but because the paschal fast begins immediately, most people think of Lent as continuing until the Easter Vigil.

3. What is the Triduum?

The paschal Triduum consists of three full *liturgical days* counted from the evening of Holy Thursday through Easter Sunday. These three days form a unified liturgical celebration, so that the Triduum may be thought of as one event extended over some seventy-two hours, marked by occasional assemblies of the faithful.

The three days are, together, the principal celebration of the paschal mystery. This means that we will find all the elements of the paschal mystery woven together, sometimes in tension with one another. We proclaim the cross in the introductory verse of Thursday evening; we affirm the resurrection in the prayers after communion on Friday; we proclaim the death of the Lord as well as his resurrection on Sunday. In short, the Triduum is not a historical drama, not a reenactment of the last days of Christ. It is the whole paschal mystery looked at from various sides.

This being said, it is also important to look at what each day of the Triduum is and what it celebrates:

1. The first day is Holy Thursday evening through Good Friday afternoon, emphasizing the Lord's passion and death.
2. The second day is Good Friday evening through Holy Saturday evening, commemorating the Lord's burial and the keeping of the great Sabbath.
3. The third day is Holy Saturday night through Easter Sunday evening, the day of the Lord's resurrection.

Before Pius XII restored the ancient Triduum observance in 1951, the liturgies of these days had moved to the morning hours and were supplemented by popular devotions of various kinds. The lenten fast was then abandoned at noon on Holy Saturday. Some people still think of the Triduum as Holy Thursday, Good Friday, and Holy Saturday, the last three days of the lenten fast.

This reckoning persists in the prohibition of Masses on Holy Thursday morning, including funeral Masses, even though Holy Thursday morning is not properly part of the Triduum.

4. What is the Easter season?

"What Sunday is to the week, the Easter season is to the year" (see *General Norms for the Liturgical Year and the Calendar* 18). In other words, the fifty days of Easter together form the annual commemoration of the Lord's resurrection. The Easter season begins with the service of light at the Easter Vigil and concludes with Evening Prayer II of Pentecost. These fifty days are also known as paschal time, the Great Sunday, or the days of Pentecost. The distinctive liturgical characteristics of these days are the singing of alleluia and the lighted Easter candle.

The Easter season is the time of mystagogical reflection and catechesis on the sacraments. The lectionary recalls the working of the Holy Spirit in the early Christian communities (Acts of the Apostles) and invites our deeper understanding of the sacramental life through the reading of John's Gospel.

5. *How is the date of Easter determined? Why do Orthodox Christians have a different date?*

The essence of the controversy over the proper day to celebrate the Lord's resurrection was: Should it coincide with the Jewish Passover (Hebrew: *Pesach*, Aramaic: *Pascha*) on the fourteenth day of the lunar month Nisan, or should it be on a Sunday, the first day of the week?

All the Gospels agree that the crucifixion, burial, and resurrection of Jesus occurred during the Passover festival (Mt 26:2,18–19, Mk 14:1–2, Lk 22:1, Jn 19:14). What is not consistent is the exact chronology. Matthew, Mark, and Luke (known as the Synoptic Gospels because of their similarities) place the Last Supper on "the first day of the feast of unleavened bread"; John notes that the crucifixion occurred as the paschal lambs were being slaughtered in preparation for the feast.

For those who are uncomfortable with such inconsistency, the following theory may be used to resolve the differences. Two different calendars were in use among the Jewish people at the time of Christ. The calendar used by the Essenes (a Jewish monastic community) and their sympathizers was a solar calendar; the "official Jewish liturgical calendar," used by the Temple priesthood, was lunar. Some suppose that Jesus celebrated the (Essene) Passover meal with his disciples on a Tuesday, then was arrested, condemned in separate trials on Wednesday and Thursday, and finally crucified on Friday, the day of preparation for the lunar or Temple Passover. Christian groups that advocated the more historical approach—that is, to celebrate the Pasch of Jesus Christ on the actual anniversary of the crucifixion/resurrection—are known as the *quartodecimans*, literally, "fourteeners." They were given this name because they kept the feast either on the fourteenth of the lunar month Nisan, the month of spring, or on its solar calendar equivalent, which in some places was set on April 6 (the fourteenth day of spring), in others, March 25 (the vernal equinox itself in those times). (For a complete explanation of this issue, see Talley 5–26.)

The Council of Nicaea (325 AD) resolved the question by decreeing that the feast of resurrection is always to be on Sunday. But the relationship of Easter to Passover and the beginning of spring was not neglected. Easter Sunday was to be celebrated on the Sunday following the first full moon (the fourteenth day of a lunar cycle) after the vernal equinox. The Council further decreed that Easter was not to coincide with Passover.

The reason Orthodox churches celebrate Easter on a different day from Roman Catholics and Protestants is that we, too, have different calendars. Western Christians use the Gregorian Calendar, so called because it was reformed by Pope Gregory XIII in 1582; Orthodox Christians continue to use the Julian Calendar (named for Julius Caesar) as the basis for their liturgical calendar. The discrepancy between the two calendars is now about thirteen days.

The Orthodox churches have established the vernal equinox (for liturgical purposes) as March 21. But March 21 on the Julian Calendar corresponds to April 3 on the common or Gregorian Calendar. So, when the Western celebration of Easter occurs on the last Sunday of March, Orthodox Easter may be almost a month later. In addition, the ancient prohibition against celebrating Easter at Passover is maintained. The difference between Julian and Gregorian calendars and the avoidance of Passover usually combine to set the date of Orthodox Easter one week after the western observance. (See also question 50.)

Lent

6. *Why do we wear ashes on Ash Wednesday when the Gospel advises us to make no outward display of religion?*

Good question. The wearing of ashes is a biblical sign of mourning and repentance (see 2 Sam 13:19, Esth 4:1, Job 42:6, 1 Macc 3:47, 4:39; Lam 2:10). By the tenth century, the giving of ashes was part of the public penitential rites of the church. Eventually all the faithful were "enrolled in the order of penitents" by receiving ashes at the beginning of Lent (Dallen 121–23).

The *Ceremonial of Bishops* notes:

> This sign of penance…expresses the human condition as affected by sin. In this sign we outwardly profess our guilt before God and thereby, prompted by the hope that the Lord is kind and compassionate, patient and abounding in mercy, express our desire for inward conversion (253).

One way to reconcile this apparent contradiction between Scripture and ritual is that we wear ashes only on one day of Lent; for the other days our fasting and penance are in secret. There is also no requirement to wear the ashes outside the liturgy. We acknowledge our sinfulness and desire for conversion among ourselves, within the community. If we accept the sign of ashes and display it publicly but do not repent, we fall under the judgment of the Gospel. It may be noted that the usual custom of signing the forehead with ashes is not mentioned in the rubrics. The crown of the head, where the chrism was received during baptism, might be suitably signed with ashes.

13

7. What is the significance of forty days?

Forty is a biblical number signifying "enough" or "ample." Forty days is another way of saying "long enough" or "enough time." The various biblical stories involving forty days all include some significant change or development in the life of the person or community: the forty days of Noah's flood (Gen 7:12), Moses on Mount Sinai for forty days until the giving of the Law (Ex 24:18), Elijah's forty-day walk through the desert to Mount Horeb (1 Kings 19:8), and Jonah's forty-day warning to the people of Nineveh (Jon 3:4). The forty-year wandering of the Israelites in the desert allowed enough time to pass for an entire generation of people to come and go; hence, a new people was born from this experience.

St. Gregory the Great (ca. 540–604) considered the six weeks of lenten weekdays, thirty-six days, as a 10-percent tithe of the year. The forty-day fast of Christ between his baptism and public ministry (Mt 4:2, Mk 1:13, Lk 4:2) is most likely the inspiration for the forty days of Lent.

8. What is fasting?

The discipline of fasting is generally understood as refraining from food and drink, or certain kinds of food and drink, for some period of time for a spiritual purpose. It is this spiritual or religious motivation that distinguishes fasting from dieting.

In the Roman Catholic tradition, fasting is quantitative; that is, the amount of food is restricted. A day of fast means that only one meal is taken; at other usual meal times, a small amount of food, not equal to a second full meal, may be eaten. Medicine or liquid may be taken at any time of day. Fast days are usually days of abstinence from meat as well.

The two required days of fast are Ash Wednesday and Good Friday. Vatican II's *Constitution on the Sacred Liturgy* (110) encourages the keeping of Holy Saturday as a day of fast as well. All other weekdays of Lent are voluntary days of fasting. According to tradition, Sundays and solemnities are never days of fast but provide a moment of refreshment in anticipation of the Great Sunday.

By contrast, Eastern Christians usually practice a qualitative fast; that is, they avoid certain kinds of foods such as meat and dairy products.

Fasting is a complex discipline and may be practiced for various reasons such as an opportunity for solidarity with the poor or as preparation for prayer. When we limit our own consumption of food, we can share more generously with others; the money we might have spent on snacks or desserts may be used to purchase items for the parish food pantry or given directly to the needy. Fasting is one way to strengthen one's willpower and serves as a way to develop other virtues in our lives.

Fasting will likely leave us tired and irritable. The physical and mental limitations imposed by a strict observance of the fast serve as a reminder of our human weakness and mortality. We may then be more humble in our relationship with God and others, more dependent on God's grace, and thus better prepared for prayer. St. Peter Chrysologus (380–450) wrote, "Fasting is the soul of prayer, mercy is the lifeblood of fasting" (Sermon on Peace 43 [Tuesday, Third Week of Lent, *Liturgy of the Hours,* vol. II, 231]). Fasting symbolizes our hunger for God; the love which motivates Christian fasting comes to life in our works of mercy and charity.

9. What is abstinence?

A bstinence is doing without or refraining from doing something. Like fasting, abstinence invites us to forego some good thing for the sake of a greater good. Abstinence during Lent refers to avoiding meat as food. Meat is traditionally understood to include the flesh of all warm-blooded animals and birds; the flesh of cold-blooded creatures such as fish, shellfish, and turtle was not considered meat. In former times all forty days of Lent were days of abstinence. In the twentieth century, the strict traditional abstinence gave way to more and more exceptions; for example, meat could be taken once a day, at the main meal, except on Fridays and Ember Days. (See question 90 for an explanation of Ember Days.)

Abstinence is obligatory on the Fridays of Lent in the United States. Abstinence is recommended on all Fridays of the year except solemnities. This voluntary abstinence is recommended by the U.S. episcopal conference on behalf of peace.[1]

---

1 See the pastoral letter of the National Conference of Catholic Bishops, *The Challenge of Peace: God's Promise and Our Response*, IV, 4.

10. What is the origin of Mardi Gras or Carnival?

Because the season of Lent was a lengthy time of fast and abstinence, it was preceded by a time known as "carnival" (derived from the Latin *carnem levare*, "to remove meat"), when the last of the forbidden foods had to be used up. This included the fats of animals used in cooking; the last day such animal fats could be used was "fat Tuesday" or *Mardi Gras* in French.

Other customs such as parades, costume balls, and public festivals date from the middle ages, although their roots may be traced to pre-Christian springtime celebrations (Weiser 166–67). People who live where winter is long and harsh naturally welcome the return of spring with its promise of more abundant food. These celebrations were later adapted to avoid conflict with the Christian season of Lent. Ironically, Mardi Gras is often celebrated by people who do not keep the lenten fast in any way; in modern times it has resumed its pagan character as a spring festival.

11. How are the main themes of Lent presented in the lectionary?

The lectionary of the lenten season is very rich and opens up for us the primary dimensions of this season, namely the call to repentance and preparation of the elect for baptism.

The Gospel of First Sunday of Lent each year is that of the temptation of Jesus in the desert; the Gospel of the Second Sunday recalls the transfiguration. The story of the temptation provides the evangelical basis for the forty-day observance and the assurance that Christ is greater than the devil and his temptations. The transfiguration story is a presage of the resurrection of the Lord. It also reflects the tradition that this event occurred forty days before the crucifixion.

On the Third, Fourth and Fifth Sundays of Lent, the Year A readings refer to the mystery of baptism and are linked to the scrutinies of the elect (see question 37). The Samaritan woman, the man born blind, and Lazarus all found new life in Christ. In Years B and C, whenever the scrutinies are celebrated on the Third, Fourth and Fifth Sundays, the Year A readings are used in place of the current cycle (at the scrutiny Mass). If there are no scrutinies, the Year B or C readings may be used on Sundays, but the Year A Gospels are then recommended as optional readings during the week. It is clear that the lectionary itself considers the narratives of the Samaritan woman, the man born blind, and Lazarus significant enough to be proclaimed every year in one way or another.

In Year B, we read the passages from John which identify the paschal mystery, particularly the cross, as the glory of Christ. First Jesus says, "Destroy this temple and in three days I will raise it up." Next he invokes the image of the serpent in the desert and says that the Son of Man must be lifted up. Finally, Jesus declares that unless the grain of wheat falls into the ground and dies it remains a single grain; his death will yield a rich harvest of believers.

In these three Sundays in Year C, Luke calls us to conversion and trust in the infinite kindness and mercy of God through the parables of the fig tree and of the two sons, and John tells the story of the woman accused of adultery. The emphasis in this year is conversion and forgiveness.

The readings of the lenten Sundays follow the principle of harmony (*Lectionary for Mass*, Introduction, 66–67). Unlike ordinary time, the first two readings and the Gospel are all meant to relate to one another. By placing these readings side by side, they actually serve as mutually interpretative texts, opening deeper meanings of the texts for the assembly. The Gospel is often presented as the fulfillment of the Old Testament and the second reading extends the mystery of Christ into the mystery of the Christian church.

On weekdays, the lenten themes of baptism and penance unfold in this way:

- The readings of Ash Wednesday and the days which follow are a call to repentance and fasting, while reminding us that fasting without almsgiving or mercy is dead. Here we see again the distinction between Lent understood as a time of penance and Lent as the season of purification and preparation for the sacraments.

- The first three weeks of Lent may be considered a basic catechesis on Christian living. The gospels are taken from the Synoptic Gospels (Matthew, Mark, or Luke) and are paired with various Old Testament narratives and prophecies in a familiar type-fulfillment pattern. In other words, the life and ministry of Jesus reflects and fulfills the persons and messages of the Old Testament. All these texts call us to fasting, prayer, repentance, forgiveness, and a renewal of our covenant with God.

- The end of the second week of Lent hints at the eventual rejection of the Son of Man by his own people.

- The fourth week of Lent begins a new set of readings. The Gospels are read from John and are meant to lead us more deeply into the mystery of Christ. This shift of emphasis is probably a remnant of the ancient, shorter Roman Lent, which actually began on Monday after our Laetare Sunday (see also question 23). In these weeks of Lent, we are

19

brought to understand the fuller significance of the
suffering and death of the Lord. The Word of God
came unto his own and his own received him not.
Even the signs of his power, such as the healing of the
official's son and of the paralyzed man at Bethesda,
are misunderstood. This rejection is part of the
glorification of the Word, who desires only to do his
Father's will, even to being lifted up on the cross. This
scriptural contemplation on the person of Christ is a
vital part of this period, called "enlightenment" in the
Rite of Christian Initiation of Adults (139). (See
question 36.)

- The Gospels of the sixth week of Lent relate some of
  the details of the Last Supper and betrayal of Jesus
  which are not included in the passion narratives. The
  first readings are from the book of the prophet Isaiah
  and are often referred to as the "songs of the servant
  of the Lord."

Homilists and catechists need prudence and sensitivity in preaching
and teaching about the conflict between Jesus and the Jewish authorities, especially in the Gospel of John, lest the apparent condemnation
of "the Jews" be taken to apply to contemporary members of the
Jewish faith. The Second Vatican Council declared:

Indeed, the church reproves every form of persecution against
whomsoever it may be directed. Remembering, then her common
heritage with the Jews and moved not by any political
consideration, but solely by the religious motivation of Christian
charity, she deplores all hatreds, persecutions, displays of
antisemitism leveled at any time or from any source against the
Jews (*Nostra Aetate* 4).

12. What are the liturgical symbols of Lent?

The fasting and purification of Lent is reflected in the austerity of the liturgy.

> In Lent the altar should not be decorated with flowers, and musical instruments may be played only to give necessary support to the singing; this is in order that the penitential character of the season be preserved (*Circular Letter* 17).

Although the primary symbols of Lent are people (the elect preparing for baptism, the penitents preparing for reconciliation, the assembly of the faithful gathered with the bishop for the so-called "stational Mass"[2]), the liturgy prescribes a few other outward signs of the season. The liturgy "fasts" from the alleluia, from flowers at the altar, and from musical instruments except to sustain the singing. The Gloria is not prayed at Sunday Mass. It is the absence of these usual liturgical practices that announces Lent to us. The violet vestments also signal the seriousness of these days. (See also question 16.) The cross, which is required to be near the altar for every liturgy, should appear more prominent in the midst of the barren sanctuary. It should not be necessary to replace the usual cross with a larger one; a second cross should never be placed in the sanctuary because a duplicated symbol weakens the impact of the symbol.

Moreover, the symbols of Lent are actions rather than things. These symbolic actions include fasting, prayer, attention to the word of God, and works of justice, mercy, and charity.

---

2 The stational Mass here refers to the ancient lenten custom of the pope celebrating Mass each day in a different church (or "station") in the diocese of Rome, to which all the faithful were invited. The sacramentary "encourages the chief shepherd of the diocese to gather his people in this way. Especially during Lent, he should meet with his people and celebrate the liturgy with them" (introduction to "Lenten Season").

13. Is there a rite for "burying the alleluia"?

In some places the word "alleluia" was written on a scroll or tablet and solemnly carried out of the church on the day before Ash Wednesday. The scroll was buried or at least hidden throughout Lent, then carried into church during the Easter Vigil. A local devotional custom, it was never taken into the official liturgy.

14. What is the meaning of veiling statues and images during Lent?

The practice of veiling began in the eleventh century with the hanging of a curtain (later known as the "hunger cloth") to screen the altar area or chancel from the penitents and even the other members of the faithful. In the next centuries, statues and images were also veiled as part of the lenten austerity, serving as a visual fast from the usually brilliantly colored iconography of the sanctuary. The veiling of images was thought to be symbolic of the Gospel which was formerly read on the Fifth Sunday of Lent, in which Jesus hides himself and withdraws from the temple (Jn 8:59). This practice was limited to the fifth and sixth weeks of Lent, then known as Passiontide.

With the revision of the liturgy after Vatican II, the episcopal conference of each country was authorized to abandon or continue the practice. In the United States, the veiling of statues has been discontinued. Parishes are not free to restore the practice on their own initiative (*Bishops' Committee on the Liturgy Newsletter* 31:14 [April 1995]).

One exception to this is that all crosses should be removed from the church after the Mass of the Lord's Supper, and any crosses which cannot be removed should be covered with a red or purple veil (*Circular Letter* 57). This permits the veneration of the cross on Good Friday to be focused on one cross.

15. What about the use of holy water during Lent? Should the font be empty?

While the sacraments of initiation are more properly celebrated at Easter, in case of need both baptism and confirmation may be celebrated during Lent, especially on Sundays. The initiation sacraments are only prohibited during the first two days of the Triduum and discouraged during Holy Week (see question 19).

Some parishes empty the baptismal font and holy water stoups during Lent to emphasize the anticipation of the Easter sacraments. Again, there is no liturgical requirement for this practice. Perhaps removing all water is an example of excessive literalism in the lenten liturgy, as though Jesus' fast in the desert is the only lenten metaphor. Some lenten Scriptures do focus on water, for example, the Gospels of the Samaritan woman and the man born blind, the healing of Naaman the leper, the "rain and snow" passage from Isaiah 55, and the life-giving water streaming from the Temple in Ezekiel's vision.

16. What kind of decorations are appropriate for Lent?

L iturgy often suffers from historicizing, that is, re-enacting, moments of the life of Christ. Lent has often been interpreted as the "last forty days of Christ's life."

Another problem is the tendency to project the mystery of the liturgy into external signs only. In other words, we focus our attention on the decoration of the building instead of on the renovation of our hearts. As the traditional practice of fasting has all but disappeared, we have turned to elaborate displays: cactus gardens, sackcloth and ashes, rough-hewn crosses complete with nails and crown of thorns. The liturgy calls for none of these.

Lent may be the ideal time to strip the church building of unnecessary accessories and clutter. The essential furnishings for Christian worship—font, table, and cross—may then appear more clearly and may need only the most discreet adornment.

Other symbols such as those mentioned above are more fitting for home, meeting room, or classroom than for the sanctuary.

17. *We used to conclude stations of the cross with benediction. Is this no longer appropriate?*

Bestowing a blessing with the eucharistic elements has a long tradition behind it. Cyril of Jerusalem (ca. 315–386) advises those who drink from the chalice to "sign themselves" with what remains on the lips after communion. From the early middle ages the sick and dying were blessed with the pyx containing the Eucharist after they had received. A similar blessing at the end of communion is a regular part of the Divine Liturgy of St. John Chrysostom. However, these blessings are always part of the eucharistic liturgy itself and serve as a solemn conclusion to the action of eating and drinking the Lord's Body and Blood (Mitchell 184).

After the development of the feast of Corpus Christi in the thirteenth century, eucharistic exposition and benediction became independent devotional services. Benediction was especially popular in times when sacramental communion was rare and Mass could be celebrated only in the morning hours. Exposition of the Blessed Sacrament and benediction immediately afterward became a common conclusion to evening devotions of all kinds. This is the reason people remember benediction as the conclusion to the stations of the cross.

The 1973 instruction *Holy Communion and Worship of the Eucharist outside Mass* affirms the ritual practice of exposition and benediction and brings it into the official liturgy of the church. At the same time it prohibits "exposition merely for the purpose of giving benediction." Benediction is understood as the conclusion of a time of worship and prayer in the presence of the Blessed Sacrament. It is not merely something to be added to another devotion.

Similarly, the stations of the cross developed from the procession of pilgrims from the traditional place of the judgment of Jesus by Pontius Pilate[3] to the Church of the Holy Sepulcher. This commemorative walk through the streets of the Old City was made available to people around the world by the placing of fourteen crosses, often with an image of the station, on the walls of the parish church. In short, the stations are best celebrated as a procession of the assembly from place to place.

Combining the stations with benediction seems to impair the spirit of both devotions.

---

3 The exact location of this site is disputed. The Gospels of Matthew and Mark refer to the Praetorium or headquarters of Pilate; John adds the detail of a courtyard called the Stone Pavement (*Gabbatha* in Hebrew, *Lithostrothos* in Greek). It may have been part of the Antonia Fortress, just north of the Temple Mount in Jerusalem, or possibly west of the Temple in one of Herod's palaces. The actual streets have not been visible since the destruction of Jerusalem in 70 AD.

18. Are weddings permitted during Lent?

The rite of marriage does not forbid weddings during Lent but reminds couples that the celebration should be consistent with the special nature of this penitential season. The customary feasting associated with weddings is difficult to harmonize with the lenten fast. Similarly, the floral decorations and festive music which are usual at church weddings are out of place during Lent.

The wedding Mass with its proper Scripture readings is not permitted on the Sundays of Lent, during Holy Week, or during the Triduum.

19. May infants be baptized during Lent?

Infants may be baptized on any day, although Sunday, the day of the Lord's resurrection, is always the preferred day (*Rite of Baptism for Children* 9). Similarly, the sacraments of initiation are preferably celebrated during the Easter season, the "Sunday" of the entire year. While not strictly prohibited, it is certainly anomalous to celebrate infant baptism at Sunday Mass during Lent. Each of the lenten Sundays is set aside for one of the adult initiation rites: the rite of sending (to the rite of election), an optional penitential rite for candidates, and the three scrutinies. Liturgically, the rites of initiation for children are derived from the adult rites; the adult order is normative. Lent is the time to prepare for baptism at Easter.

In case of necessity, of course, infants may be baptized during Lent, but it is more suitable that infant baptism be deferred until Easter.

In addition, the *Circular Letter* states that "it is not fitting that Baptisms and Confirmations be celebrated" on Passion Sunday through Holy Thursday" (27).

29

20. What are our options for penance services?

L ent is the primary penitential season in the Catholic Church. As such, every opportunity should be made available to celebrate the mystery of conversion and reconciliation. The *Circular Letter* addresses the needs of uncatechized adults and unbaptized children as well as of the whole community of the faithful, for a deeper spirit of penance:

> In Lent there should be catechesis for those adults who, although baptized when infants, were not brought up in the faith and consequently have not been confirmed nor have they received the Eucharist. During this period penitential services should be arranged to help prepare them for the sacrament of Reconciliation.
>
> The lenten season is also an appropriate time for the celebration of penitential rites on the model of the scrutinies for unbaptized children, who are at an age to be catechized, and also for children already baptized, before being admitted to the sacrament of penance.
>
> The virtue and practice of penance form a necessary part of the preparation for Easter. From that inner conversion of heart should spring the practice of penance, both for the individual Christian and of the whole community which, while being adapted to the conditions of the present time, should nevertheless witness to the evangelical spirit of penance and also be to the advantage of others.
>
> The role of the Church in penitential practices is not to be neglected, and encouragement is to be given to pray for sinners; this intention should be included in the prayer of the faithful.
>
> The faithful are to be encouraged to participate in an ever more intense and fruitful way in the lenten liturgy and in penitential celebrations. They are to be clearly reminded that both according to the law and tradition, they should approach the sacrament of Penance during this season, so that with purified heart they may participate in the paschal mysteries. It is appropriate that during Lent the sacrament of Penance be celebrated according to the rite for the reconciliation of several penitents with individual

confession and absolution, as given in the Roman Ritual. Pastors should devote themselves to the ministry of reconciliation and provide sufficient time for the faithful to avail themselves of this sacrament (9–10, 14–15).

What is envisioned here is much more than extra hours for individual confessions. Lent provides a fitting time for adult education in areas of ethics, moral theology, and conscience formation as well as liturgical catechesis (the meaning of the sacramental rites), drawn from the Scriptures and other primary sources of Catholic tradition.

Lent is also a time for penitential celebrations: ritual prayer (for example, a Liturgy of the Word) on themes such as election, covenant, sin (social and personal), conversion, repentance, atonement, forgiveness, reconciliation, communion. Such celebrations do not of themselves include the sacrament of penance but serve as preparation for it. These services may be arranged in a progressive series or as a parish mission, culminating in the *Rite of Penance*, form II, the reconciliation of several penitents with individual confession and absolution. Ecumenical prayer celebrations should not be overlooked. Interfaith dialogue, education, or responses to local community needs are also possibilities.

The *Circular Letter* also speaks of the "practice of penance." Penitential practices are not limited to prayer services. Fasting may be ritualized by gathering for an evening meal of bread and broth, with a collection of food and money for the poor. Gatherings for action on behalf of justice; providing food, clothing and shelter; assisting the undereducated; organizing visits to the homebound and outreach to the alienated—the possibilities are limited only by our creativity. All these works of mercy may be "practiced" during Lent in the hope that they will be integrated into normal Christian life by Easter.

The rite of penance includes three forms of reconciliation. The third form, commonly known as general absolution, requires the permission of the diocesan bishop. The policy of the local diocese must be followed in this regard.

Lent will also serve as the ritual completion of the process of reconciliation for those who have been alienated from the church. Pastoral opportunities such as Re-membering Church and similar outreach ministries need to be considered when planning the lenten penitential rites.

21. How are saints' days celebrated during Lent?

One of the goals of the 1969 calendar reform was to allow the celebrations of the principal mysteries of salvation, for example, those relating to the incarnation or the Lord's passion, to have priority. Celebrations in honor of the saints were ranked as solemnities, feasts, memorials, and optional memorials. As much as possible, saints' days were relocated to other appropriate days outside of Lent. For example, the memorial of St. Gregory the Great was transferred from March 12, the date of his death, to September 3, the date of his election as pope.

Obligatory memorials remaining in February, March, and early April are kept only as "commemorations" during Lent. In other words, the readings and Mass prayers of the lenten weekday take priority; only the opening prayer of the saint may be used.

Feasts and solemnities are celebrated with the liturgical texts assigned to them. If a solemnity occurs on a Sunday of Lent, it is celebrated on the preceding Saturday; if it occurs during Holy Week it is celebrated after the octave of Easter. If a feast or memorial occurs on a Sunday or during Holy Week, it is not celebrated.

22. Is the Liturgy of the Hours different during Lent?

The Liturgy of the Hours during Lent uses the same arrangement of psalms as during the rest of the year. Readings, responses, antiphons for the Canticles of Zechariah and of Mary, intercessions, and concluding prayers are proper to each day of Lent. The main difference is that all the memorials of the saints are superseded by the weekdays of Lent.

When a saint is commemorated, an antiphon and prayer honoring the saint may be said in place of the conclusion of the proper prayer of the day.

For example, if Wednesday of the third week of Lent occurs on March 17, St. Patrick's Day, the conclusion of Morning Prayer is:

> Lord, during this lenten season,
> nourish us with your word of life
> and make us one in faith and prayer.
> *Go, and teach all nations,*
> *baptizing them in the name of the Father,*
> *and of the Son and of the Holy Spirit.*
> God our Father, you sent Saint Patrick
> to preach your glory to the people of Ireland.
> By the help of his prayers,
> may all Christians proclaim your love to all men.
> Grant this through our Lord Jesus Christ, your Son,
> who lives and reigns with you and the Holy Spirit,
> one God, for ever and ever. Amen (emphasis added).

This rather complex combination of texts works if the hour is sung and the antiphon has some proper melody to distinguish it from the collects which surround it. This type of commemoration should be a rare occurrence—for example, to honor the patron of the parish or diocese.

For the Office of Readings, the hymn of praise (known by its Latin title *Te Deum*) is not used on Sundays in Lent; the Gospels of the resurrection are replaced by texts predicting the Lord's passion. If a saint is commemorated on a weekday, the reading proper to the saint may be read only after the two readings assigned to the day.

23. What is Laetare Sunday?

The Fourth Sunday of Lent, so named from the first word of the Latin entrance antiphon *Laetare, Ierusalem*, "Rejoice, Jerusalem" (Isa 66:10), is a remnant of the ancient Roman observance of only three weeks of fasting before Easter. Laetare Sunday was thus the last day before the fasting time began. It was customary to bring roses to church on that day and give them to the elect, thus the association of this Sunday with roses and eventually the rose-colored vestments.

Laetare Sunday is the only Sunday of Lent when the Roman liturgy officially permits flowers at the altar and instrumental music.

Because the rose vestments were always optional, Laetare Sunday was not consistently observed throughout the church and has generally fallen into disuse since Vatican II. Because the Fourth Sunday of Lent is one of the scrutiny Sundays, our attention is fittingly directed to prayer for the elect rather than how quickly the days of Lent are passing by. Nonetheless, Laetare Sunday is a reminder of the spirit of joy which touches every Sunday of Lent. The short reading for Sunday Morning Prayer reminds us each week:

> "Today is holy to the LORD your God. Do not be sad, and do not weep; for today is holy to our LORD. Do not be saddened this day, for rejoicing in the LORD must be your strength!"
> (Neh 8:9–10).

24. What is Passiontide?

Passiontide refers to the last two weeks of Lent in the former Roman calendar. During this time images and crosses were veiled. Passiontide as a separate part of Lent was discontinued with the 1969 reform of the calendar.

The two Sundays in the old Passiontide were called "Passion Sunday" and "Palm Sunday." In the current calendar, what had been "Passion Sunday" is now the Fifth Sunday of Lent; "Passion Sunday" is now the preferred name for Palm Sunday because the more important element is the proclamation of the Passion Gospel rather than the blessing of palms. The Latin name for this Sixth Sunday of Lent is *Dominica in palmis de passione Domini*, literally "Sunday in Palms of the Passion of the Lord." Most calendars simply list the two names together as "Passion (Palm) Sunday."

25. What is Holy Week?

Holy Week is the sixth week of Lent. It includes Passion Sunday (Palm Sunday) and the days which follow it, until the beginning of the paschal Triduum. The days of Holy Week take precedence over all other celebrations.

26. What is the Chrism Mass?

A t this Mass, traditionally celebrated on Holy Thursday morning, the holy oils are blessed for use in the sacraments, especially the sacraments of initiation. The bishop presides together with the presbyterate of the diocese. In places where it is difficult for the clergy to gather just before the Triduum, the Chrism Mass may be celebrated some days earlier. Because the presbyterate gathers for the blessing of the oils, and because Holy Thursday is associated with the institution of the ministerial priesthood, the Chrism Mass has also become the setting for the rite of renewal of commitment to priestly service. This renewal rite first appeared in the 1974 sacramentary; it was created in response to the Holy See's concern about the number of priests who resigned from the active ministry during the 1960s.

In the rite of blessing the oils, three vessels of oil, usually olive oil, are presented to the bishop. One is for the oil of the sick; the second is for the oil of catechumens; the third, mixed with balsam or other fragrances, is consecrated as sacred chrism. The ancient Roman custom was to bless the oil of the sick before the end of the eucharistic prayer; the blessing of the oil of catechumens and the consecration of the chrism took place after communion. The present rite provides for all three blessings to take place immediately after the Liturgy of the Word and the renewal of commitment to priestly service.

| 27. | *Why is the feast of the Annunciation (March 25) celebrated after Easter some years?* |

When March 25 occurs during Holy Week, the Triduum, or the octave of Easter, the solemnity of the Annunciation of the Lord is transferred to the next available day which is not a solemnity, namely, Monday of the second week of Easter.

28. May a funeral take place during the Triduum?

A funeral Mass may not be celebrated on Holy Thursday, Good Friday, Holy Saturday, or Easter Sunday. When someone dies during or just prior to this time, there are some options. One option is to delay the entire order of funeral rites until Easter Monday. When this is not possible or desirable, a funeral liturgy (without Mass) may be celebrated in the parish church or other suitable place, such as the chapel of the mortuary or cemetery. This funeral liturgy should include the elements of receiving the body, a complete Liturgy of the Word including homily and intercessions, and the rites of commendation and farewell. The rite of committal is celebrated at the place of interment as usual. A memorial Eucharist may then be celebrated after Easter Sunday. Holy communion is not permitted at a funeral liturgy during the Triduum.

29. What are the proper liturgical colors of these days?

The Mass of the Lord's Supper and the entire Easter Vigil are celebrated with white vestments; the Liturgy of the Lord's Passion is celebrated with red Mass vestments.

Red is also the color for the Liturgy of the Hours on Good Friday; on Holy Saturday, violet is used for the Liturgy of the Hours and the preparation rites for the catechumens.

30. Are there any restrictions on music during Lent and Triduum?

The *Ceremonial of Bishops* and the *Circular Letter* advise that musical instruments be played only to sustain the singing. Instrumental music alone or embellished accompaniments are preferably kept for the time of Easter rejoicing.

This need not be taken in a rigid, legalistic sense, as though all music is prohibited. Music expresses a wide range of emotions and can evoke various responses. Parish musicians should consider how best to convey the desired sense of penitence and austerity through music. A solo instrument may well serve to establish a more reflective atmosphere in a church that is otherwise noisy.

31. What aspects of the Rite of Christian Initiation of Adults are proper to Lent?

One of the roots of Lent is the preparation of catechumens for baptism, confirmation and eucharist. In ancient times, those to be baptized were asked to fast and pray; inquiry was made among the members of the community as to the readiness of the catechumens. The time of fasting varied from two days to three weeks or more before developing into its present forty-day structure.

The Second Vatican Council ordered that the baptismal elements of Lent be restored (*Constitution on the Sacred Liturgy* 109a). *The Rite of Christian Initiation of Adults* indicates that Lent is the proper time for the period of purification and enlightenment of the elect, that is, those who have completed the period of catechesis and are ready for the sacraments (see question 36).

In addition, for those who are to be baptized at Easter, the rite of election, the scrutinies, and the presentations of the creed and of the Lord's Prayer are celebrated during Lent.

32. What is the rite of election?

The rite of election celebrates the choice of the catechumens for the Easter sacraments. This rite signifies that God, through Christ and his church, in the person of the diocesan bishop, has chosen those catechumens who have been converted to Christ, have accepted the teaching of the church, have given evidence of their new way of life, and have joined the community in faith and prayer. In simpler terms: At the beginning of the catechumenate, the catechumens express their desire to join our church; at the time of election, the church approves this desire and decides that the catechumens are ready for baptism.

Because it assures the catechumens that they will be baptized at the next Easter Vigil, the rite of election is a significant event in the life of the whole church. The bishop should receive testimony from the sponsors, catechists, and others in the community about the readiness of the catechumens. Part of this readiness involves being sure that no obstacle exists to the reception of the sacraments; for example, marriage cases and other canonical procedures should be resolved favorably before proceeding to the rite of election.

The Rite of Election marks the end of the period of catechesis. The catechumens are henceforth known as "the elect." The rite of election also begins the period of purification and enlightenment which normally coincides with Lent; the proper day for the rite of election is the First Sunday of Lent. If this is not possible, another day near the beginning of Lent may be chosen.

Ordinarily this rite is celebrated as a diocesan event, that is, by the bishop personally or his delegate, at the cathedral church or another prominent local church, or, because of the size of the assembly, another suitable place (*Rite of Christian Initiation of Adults* 122, 127).

The rite of election also marks the beginning of the ministry of the godparents. It may happen that the catechumen chooses his or her sponsor to serve as godparent. The distinction between sponsor and godparent is sometimes explained in terms of the duration of the commitment. A sponsor is ordinarily chosen by the community and assists the catechumen through the period of catechumenate; a parish may have a relatively stable corps of sponsors who serve year after year. On the other hand, the godparent is chosen by the catechumen and remains a spiritual companion and guide for the rest of his or her life. The rite of election is also known as the rite of enrollment:

> The step is also called the enrollment of names because as a pledge of fidelity the candidates inscribe their names in the book that lists those who have been chosen for initiation (RCIA 119).

It is important that this step not be confused with the rite of acceptance into the catechumenate. The rite of acceptance, which is followed by the recording of the names of the newly admitted catechumens in a register (RCIA 46), is the beginning of the catechumenate, whereas election marks the end of the catechumenal period.

33. Why is the bishop the presiding celebrant of the rite of election?

The Second Vatican Council emphasizes the pastoral ministry of the bishop:

> The bishop is to be looked on as the high priest of his flock, the faithful's life in Christ in some way deriving from and dependent on him.
> Therefore all should hold in great esteem the liturgical life of the diocese centered around the bishop, especially in his cathedral church… (*Constitution on the Sacred Liturgy* 41).

> In the bishops, therefore, for whom priests are assistants, Our Lord Jesus Christ, the Supreme High Priest, is present in the midst of those who believe.…He incorporates new members in His Body by a heavenly regeneration, and finally by their wisdom and prudence He directs and guides the People of the New Testament in their pilgrimage toward eternal happiness. These pastors, chosen to shepherd the Lord's flock of the elect, are servants of Christ and stewards of the mysteries of God… (*Dogmatic Constitution on the Church* 20–21.)

The diocesan bishop is properly the presider of all the sacraments of initiation. This is generally not practical. To manifest in some way his pastoral care for all those to be initiated, the bishop will preside at the rite of election for the entire diocese, administer the sacraments of initiation during the Easter Vigil at which he presides, and gather the newly baptized during the Easter season for the celebration of the Eucharist (RCIA 12, 251; canon 863; *National Statutes* 11).

When even this level of involvement is not possible, the bishop may delegate someone else to receive the testimony about the catechumens and to choose them for the sacraments in his name.

34. Are candidates also elected?

The word "candidate" is short for "candidate for reception into the full communion of the Catholic Church." A candidate is a baptized Christian and therefore already a member of the assembly of the faithful. Election, as we have seen, refers to the choosing of a person by God and the church for baptism, and so candidates cannot be elected. The full Rite of Christian Initiation of Adults is only for those who are unbaptized. While some "elements of catechumenal formation" may be appropriate for those candidates who have received little or no Christian upbringing, they "should not take part in rites intended for unbaptized catechumens" (*National Statutes for the Catechumenate* 31).

There is no doubt that the catechesis based on the word of God which is the heart of the catechumenate period is also of great benefit to the candidates and even the fully initiated Catholics who may take part in it. It is also likely that bonds of community and friendship will develop among catechumens and candidates as they reflect on the Scriptures and share their diverse journeys into faith. Unfortunately, these gifts are understood by some pastoral ministers as constituting catechumens and candidates alike into "a convert class." The image of "a class" and the indiscriminate use of the word "convert" should be rejected. "Converts" are actually those who have moved from unbelief to faith, not baptized Christians who have changed denominations.

While the rites of adult initiation are designed for the unbaptized, secondary (and optional) rites have also been developed for use in the dioceses of the United States so that both catechumens and candidates may mark their faith journeys in preparation for the Eucharist. There is a rite which may be celebrated at the same time as the rite of election, the *call to continuing conversion*. This rite affirms the baptismal dignity of the candidates and invites them to take full part in the lenten observance of the Catholic Church.

35. *Whose names are inscribed in the Book of the Elect?*

The names of those who are actually elected or chosen for the Easter sacraments in a given year are written in the Book of the Elect. This enrollment of names (see question 32) serves as an announcement to the parish community of those who are to be baptized. The inscribed names may also be presented to the local bishop during the rite of election.

Again, candidates' names are not properly written in the Book of the Elect.

36. What is "purification and enlightenment?"

These terms are used to describe the process of spiritual growth or development emphasized during the lenten season. "Illumination" or "enlightenment" is an ancient term for baptism itself:

> For once you were darkness, but now in the Lord you are light. Live as children of the light—for the fruit of the light is found in all that is good and right and true (Eph 5:8–9).

The Letter to the Hebrews also uses the image of purification for the forgiveness of sins which baptism obtains for us:

> When [Christ] had made purification for sins... (Heb 1:3).

> [L]et us approach with a true heart in full assurance of faith, with our hearts sprinkled clean from an evil conscience and our bodies washed with pure water (Heb 10:22).

The terms "purification" and "enlightenment" are now used for the final period of preparation for baptism. The intent of the *Rite of Christian Initiation of Adults* is that Lent is:

> a period of more intense spiritual preparation, consisting more in interior reflection than in catechetical instruction, and is intended to purify the minds and hearts of the elect as they search their own consciences and do penance. This period is intended as well to enlighten the minds and hearts of the elect with a deeper knowledge of Christ the Savior (RCIA 139).

Lent is not the time merely to study or talk about sin and grace but a time to see for ourselves how sin and grace are at work within us. The catechist is replaced by a spiritual guide who can help each of the elect to discern the presence of the Holy Spirit within, the Spirit who both convicts us of sin (1 Cor 14:24–25; Jn 16:8) and assures us of God's forgiveness in Christ, the Spirit who teaches us how to pray (Rom 8:26–27) and how to acknowledge Jesus the Lord (1 Cor 12:3).

37. What is a scrutiny? What is an exorcism?

A scrutiny is an examination or investigation; in the rites of initiation, the candidate goes through three scrutinies so that the presence of sin may be unmasked and the power and mercy of Jesus Christ revealed. The rite itself describes this aptly:

> The scrutinies are meant to uncover, then heal all that is weak, defective or sinful in the hearts of the elect; to bring out, then strengthen all that is upright, strong and good (RCIA 141).

In ancient times the exorcist was trained to recognize bodily manifestations of the presence of the devil, hence the image of examination. This may seem ridiculous to modern people. Nevertheless, we too accept the interaction of body and spirit; we acknowledge psychosomatic illness and look for genetic predispositions to what were once thought only mental illnesses. The current rites obviously do not expect this kind of expertise of the minister of initiation. What is required is a willingness to help people examine their own consciences in the form of a genuine spiritual inventory or review of life. This is much more than a simple listing of sins. The elect may have to confront for the first time the truth about his or her previous way of life. If issues are surfaced that require more attention, the elect should be promptly referred to those who can provide the necessary pastoral care or professional assistance.

An exorcism is a prayer to God asking that the person be freed from the power of evil. One kind of exorcism (unfortunately, the only kind most people think of when they hear the word "exorcism") is a rite used in the case of demonic possession and requires an explicit delegation by the bishop (canon 1172). Another kind is the "minor exorcism," which is the prayer for liberation from evil offered during the catechumenate (RCIA 79, 90–94). These rites anticipate and prepare the catechumen for the healing and strengthening effect of the lenten scrutinies. The scrutinies are yet another kind of exorcism, for in them the entire assembly prays that the elect be liberated from sin and all the power of evil.

The "order of exorcist," once one of the four minor orders (distinct steps in the preparation of seminarians for the priesthood), was abolished in 1972; deacons and priests are authorized to perform the minor exorcisms of the rites of initiation in virtue of their ordination. The bishop may also depute worthy catechists to celebrate the minor exorcisms and blessings (RCIA 34:5).

38. Do the candidates also participate in the scrutinies?

The purpose of the scrutinies is the preparation of the elect for baptism. Because the candidates for reception into the full communion of the Catholic Church are already baptized Christians, the scrutinies with their exorcisms and prayer for the elect are not appropriate. The one baptism we profess "for the forgiveness of sins" is also the candidate's liberation from the powers of evil.

Those non-Catholic Christians who have come to a renewal of their baptismal faith in the context of the initiation process may be invited to a penitential rite which is optional on the Second Sunday of Lent.

39. What are the presentations?

The presentations are the solemn ritual handing on of the summary of the church's prayer and belief in the form of the Lord's Prayer and the Apostle's Creed.

These rites are reminiscent of the times when people learned prayers and other texts by rote. The Lord's Prayer and Apostle's Creed were recited by the catechist and repeated by the catechumens.

The creed is presented during the week following the First Scrutiny (the third week of Lent). The Lord's Prayer is presented during the week following the Third Scrutiny (the fifth week of Lent) (RCIA 157–63; 178–84).

In the present rite, when the creed is presented, the presider of the Mass or Liturgy of the Word gives a homily on the Scriptures provided for the occasion. The elect are then invited to listen as the presider and assembly recite the creed. They then pray for the elect and dismiss them. The elect do not repeat the creed at this time; the recitation of the creed may take place during the preparation rites on Holy Saturday (RCIA 193–96).

When the Lord's Prayer is presented, the elect are called forward for the reading of the Gospel which contains the prayer. The homily, prayer over the elect, and dismissal follow.

Some communities also present the texts of the creed and the Lord's Prayer in printed form for study and reflection by the elect. In this case, the living tradition (literally, "handing on") of the creed and the Lord's Prayer by the assembly should take place first.

40.	What is the meaning of the oil of catechumens?

The oil of catechumens is used to anoint catechumens whenever this seems beneficial or desirable (RCIA 98) during the time of their formation, usually one year in duration (*National Statutes* 6). As with all the rites of initiation, the anointing should ritualize the conversion which is actually taking place. It celebrates some progress in the journey of initiation and manifests a new reality at work in the person's life.

The oil of catechumens is blessed by the bishop at the Mass but may also be blessed by a priest celebrant on the occasion of the anointing. This oil is described in the rite:

> The anointing with oil symbolizes their need for God's help and strength so that, undeterred by the bonds of the past and overcoming the opposition of the devil, they will forthrightly take the step of professing their faith and will hold fast to it unfalteringly throughout their lives (RCIA 99).

The oil of catechumens has been compared to the olive oil used by ancient athletes and wrestlers to strengthen and prepare their bodies for the contest. The catechumen is anointed in preparation for the spiritual struggle against sin and evil. The catechumen is also re-minded that it is Jesus Christ who is the victorious one.

In the dioceses of the United States, the oil of catechumens is reserved for use during the catechumenate and during the period of purification and enlightenment. It is not to be used on Holy Saturday nor during the Easter Vigil (RCIA 33.7; *National Statutes* 16.) The reasons for this restriction are not clear; perhaps it is meant to prevent confusion between the anointing with the oil of catechumens and the use of chrism in the sacraments of initiation.

Triduum

41. When does the Triduum begin?

The opening of the Triduum is the evening Mass of the Lord's Supper. No specific time is stated for this liturgy. The first day of the Triduum, following the ancient Jewish reckoning of time, should begin at sunset. The local custom for the time of vigil Masses may be used, or a later hour may be chosen.

Evening Prayer is not celebrated, except by those who do not participate in the evening Mass.

42. What is meant by "Maundy Thursday?"

The English word "maundy" is derived from the Latin *mandatum*, or "commandment." Since Christ gave the "new commandment" of mutual love during the Last Supper farewell discourse, the celebration of the Lord's Supper includes the commemoration of the mandatum. The term *mandatum* is also used to refer to the ritual of the washing of the feet (see question 44).

43. What are the main elements of the Mass of the Lord's Supper?

The Mass of the Lord's Supper is the beginning of the paschal Triduum. This Mass includes the usual elements of the introductory rites (including the Gloria, during which the church bells may be rung), Liturgy of the Word and Liturgy of the Eucharist. In addition to these, the Mass may include the *mandatum* or washing of feet and an optional presentation of the holy oils blessed by the bishop. In place of the concluding rites, there is a procession to transfer the Blessed Sacrament to the place of reservation.

We begin the Triduum with a solemn celebration of Eucharist while focusing on the table ritual by which Jesus willed to be remembered. We do this not as a re-enactment of the Last Supper but with the words and ceremonies which our church has developed to continue the tradition. This is liturgy, not theater. *This* is what *we do* "in memory" of him.

A comment about the Christian understanding of memory or remembrance is appropriate here. The English word "memory" is barely equivalent to the Greek "anamnesis," which means a calling to mind in such a way that the mystery is truly present to us and we enter into it. We do not simply think about the mystery; we live anew the saving events of the life of Christ. Unlike the "mysteries" of pagan belief which provided entry into an endless cycle of myths about personified forces of nature and imagined gods and goddesses, the Christian mysteries are rooted in actual human history. Nevertheless, the impact of the Christian mysteries transcends all history. Louis Bouyer writes:

> The Mystery, therefore, is an action; and it is an action which took place in the past and can never be repeated, because it is perfect. The Mystery is the cross of Jesus....This action is as it were the inner essence of the Mystery. But the Mystery is permanently embodied in the liturgy—more especially in the Mass, but also in all the sacraments and even in the sacramentals,

in the Divine Office, in the feasts of the liturgical year, and in the whole Christian life....In all this, of course, the Mystery is hidden. Nothing is present of the historical circumstances by which the divine action was set in its place in time and space. But the substance of the action is present, in a mysterious way, entirely real to faith... (87–88).

An appreciation of how the historical event (for example, the Last Supper or the crucifixion) still engages us in our liturgical celebration is what separates dramatizing that history (as in a passion play) from participating in the mystery (the eucharistic liturgy).

44. What is the significance of the mandatum or footwashing?

The Gospel of John does not describe the institution of the Eucharist during his narrative of the Last Supper. Instead, Jesus, knowing that now is the hour for his passover from this world to the Father, gives his last instructions to the disciples. Within the setting of the meal, Jesus imposes a dual command: to wash one another's feet and to love one another.

As in every sacramental rite, the words specify what the gesture means in a specific instance. (For example, several sacraments include the laying on of hands, but the accompanying prayer makes it clear whether the gesture is forgiveness, ordination, healing, and so on.) In John 13, the commandment of love specifies the meaning of the footwashing gesture: love for one another. In the synoptic Gospels, Jesus gives his life symbolically at the table and in reality on the cross. The cross and the table ritual are one gift. In John, Jesus washes his disciples' feet as a gesture of love; this love is his glory as he is lifted up on the cross.

45. Who may participate in the mandatum rite?

How we understand the rite itself will help us decide the appropriate participants. We may look at the mandatum as a historical representation of the Gospel narrative. The participants will then be viewed as portraying the apostles; their participation in the ritual connotes also the command to "do this in memory of me," that is, to celebrate the Eucharist. Simply, the apostles' participation in the Last Supper is equated in the minds of most Catholics with the institution of the priesthood. It is likely that the rubrics speak of *viri selecti* (chosen men) from this perspective. Some parishioners will be offended if anyone not qualified for ordination is brought forward for the *mandatum*. Remember, ritual communicates meaning.

If the *mandatum* is viewed instead as a ritualizing of mutual love as commanded by the Lord Jesus, the rite will tend toward including various members of the parish, who may also in turn wash the feet of other members.

At the time of this writing, the U.S. bishops' conference has prepared a pastoral introduction to the order of the Mass. This document recommends that those invited to the mandatum ceremony be a representative group of the entire assembly. The presider leads the rite but is not the only one to wash feet. In this view, washing feet or being washed is not related at all to the sacrament of holy orders but to the sacrament of baptism and the discipleship it covenants.

It should also be noted that the mandatum is not performed during the reading of the Gospel.

…

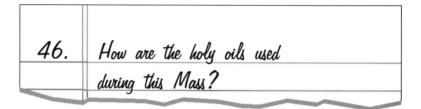

46. How are the holy oils used during this Mass?

In 1989 an optional rite was approved for the reception of the holy oils which were blessed at the Chrism Mass. The oils may be presented at the altar during the procession of the gifts. Prayers of thanksgiving are said which parallel the prayers of preparation of the bread and wine. The oils are then taken to their place of reservation.

It is difficult to understand the value of this rite, since the oils themselves are not used during the Mass of the Lord's Supper. The addition of this ritual element may actually diminish the liturgy. Parish ministers should implement the rite only after careful consideration.

47. *Our parish priests renewed their ordination vows at this Mass last year. Is this something new?*

When the bishop gathers with his presbyterate for the Chrism Mass, the priests are invited to renew their commitment to priestly ministry. This renewal should never be understood as though sacramental ordination is a renewable contract with the church. It is rather an invitation to remember the promises of service made at the time of ordination and a request for mutual prayer and support among bishop, presbyters, and all the faithful.

There is no provision to repeat this rite during the Mass of the Lord's Supper. The liturgy of the Triduum is rich enough and should not be complicated with unnecessary rites.

More importantly, the entrance into the paschal Triduum should not be complicated by attempting to celebrate "the anniversary of the institution of the priesthood." The ministerial priesthood is one of the three recommended themes for the homily at this Mass, but this reference to priesthood needs to be kept in balance with the other emphases of the evening's liturgy (commandment of love and institution of the Eucharist) and of the entire Triduum. A tendency to clericalize the liturgy is hard to break, even when it is the well-meant affirmation of hard-working pastors.

48. *What is meant by the paschal fast?*
How is the paschal fast distinct
from the lenten fast?

The paschal fast refers to the days of fasting immediately before the celebration of the Lord's resurrection. The earliest tradition called for a fast of two days (Good Friday and Holy Saturday) when the bridegroom has been taken from us (Mt 9:15). This developed into a "paschal fast" during the six days of Holy Week.

The lenten fast is ascetical, emphasizing self-discipline and penance. The paschal fast is one of anticipation and preparation. The paschal fast may be compared to the way in which we forget to eat (or cannot eat) when we are too busy, upset, in mourning, or excited. We have other things on our minds and we do not stop to eat.

Another (usually overlooked) aspect of the paschal fast is that it is communal. Unlike the lenten fast which may be observed voluntarily and to the extent desired by an individual or family, the paschal fast is a community event. Ideally the whole parish supports one another in keeping these days holy.

49. *May communion be given during the Triduum apart from Mass or liturgical services?*

On Holy Thursday and Good Friday the Eucharist may be brought to the sick at any time. On Holy Saturday, communion may be given only as viaticum, the last participation in the Eucharist by a dying person.

Otherwise, sharing in sacramental communion is limited to the Mass of the Lord's Supper, the liturgy of the passion of the Lord, and the Easter Vigil Mass. Other "communion services" are not permitted.

50. Should Christians celebrate Passover?

This is a difficult and complex issue. The relationship of Passover and Easter was explored in question 5. It is also important to consider the relationship of Passover to the Eucharist.

It is simplistic to assume that the Last Supper was the Passover seder meal (as we know it today) and that therefore the Passover seder is the "original form" of the Christian Eucharist. These assumptions have led Catholic parish ministers to perform the seder ritual, sometimes freely adapting it, changing the order of elements to match Christian ritual practice, and making explicit references to Jesus Christ in the course of the meal. While this may have a few catechetical advantages, there are some serious disadvantages, not the least of which is the questionable practice of appropriating the sacred ritual of another faith community. (Would Catholics appreciate it if the ritual of the Mass was performed by non-Christians?)

The question of Christians celebrating Passover needs to be answered on three levels: historical, liturgical, and interfaith.

Historical. The question of whether the Last Supper was actually a Passover meal has long been debated. As noted in question 5, one might assume two distinct Passover observances so that the Gospel narratives will harmonize. It is certain that the Lord's death and resurrection occurred at Passover time. Exactly what the Last Supper meal consisted of is not entirely clear. For example, the Gospel of Mark notes that the celebration took place "on the first day of the feast of unleavened bread," yet the narrative goes on to say that Jesus said the blessing over ordinary bread (*artos*), not the unleavened bread (*azymes*) required for the feast. Was this a slip of the pen or was Mark recounting the form of the Christian eucharistic liturgy into the Last Supper narrative?

No Gospel describes the ritual in detail; only the basic tradition is recounted. Jesus took bread, said the blessing, broke the bread, and gave it to them. After the meal he took the cup, said the blessing, and gave it to them. Even here there are disparities. The exact words differ between the tradition preserved by Matthew and Mark and that of Luke and Paul.

Given these questions, it is difficult to advocate celebrating the Passover seder as a reenactment of the last supper.

Liturgical. Similarly, the liturgical issues must be addressed. The first generations of Christians adapted their worship from both Jewish and gentile practices, carefully eliminating anything which was contrary to the Christian Gospel but remaining rooted in their own culture. At the same time, the destruction of the Temple in Jerusalem and the dispersion of the Jews necessitated changes in the Jewish celebration of Passover. Judaism did not cease to develop once the Christian church became an independent body. The seder as it exists today has evolved somewhat from its ancient form.

Even if the Last Supper was the Passover meal as Jesus knew it, we need to remember that the ancient eucharistic liturgy of the house churches had already developed beyond the Last Supper, as Justin the Martyr (ca. 150) describes.

While we "do this in memory of" Jesus, we do not do exactly as Jesus did. The order of the eucharistic liturgy has evolved generation after generation to meet the needs of its time. The Liturgy of the Word is partly derived from the synagogue liturgy of the first centuries, but is not identical to it. Nor was the synagogue service of Scripture readings and prayers ever incorporated into the Passover seder. The concept of a sacrificial meal is found in both Jewish and gentile sources. Even the language of atoning sacrifice is closer to the Yom Kippur (Day of Atonement) liturgy than to the Passover. The seder and the Eucharist bear witness to both the preservation of the tradition and its adaptation.

A more significant point of the question is why Christians might want to celebrate the Jewish Passover. As the Exsultet proclaims during the Easter Vigil:

> This is our passover feast, when Christ, the true Lamb, is slain, whose blood consecrates the homes of all believers.

The "passover feast" of Christians is nothing less than the Easter Eucharist.

On the other hand, the value of celebrating the Passover seder for Christians is simply that we cannot appreciate "our passover feast" if we have no idea what a "passover" is. It is also increasingly difficult to initiate people into a ritual meal in an era when ritual dining has all but disappeared. The Jewish seder meal is an excellent model of how dining together can be framed by religious ritual and focused on sharing faith experience. Christians have much to learn from this tradition.

Nevertheless, Catholics and other Christians do have traditions of religious meal sharing, including the use of blessed food. We need not go outside our own faith tradition in order to recover some of the lost values of ritual dining.

Interfaith. The interfaith question is equally important. If Christians, for the sake of mutual understanding, wish to celebrate the seder meal with their Jewish neighbors, the best approach would be to attend the celebration in a Jewish home or with a Jewish congregation which may have a "congregational seder" for the benefit of their members who are unable to celebrate with family. In some areas, the Jewish community may welcome such participation as a means of encouraging good relations among Jews and Christians. This approach respects the seder as a Jewish religious ritual.

Materials are available for Christians to study the seder ritual and celebrate it among themselves. Again, these celebrations should remain faithful to the Jewish tradition. The seder meal cannot replace or overshadow the Triduum and its liturgies, for in these rites we celebrate Jesus Christ as our passover. As the apostle Paul reminds us, "our paschal lamb, Christ, has been sacrificed" (1 Cor 5:7).

51. What is the Easter duty?

The Fourth Lateran Council (1215) decreed that Catholics must partake of the sacrament of holy communion at least once a year and at Easter. For those aware of serious sin, sacramental confession and absolution are required before this communion, hence the popular understanding that everyone must go to confession and communion during Eastertime: the "Easter duty."

The 1917 *Code of Canon Law* specified the time for the Easter communion as the days from Palm Sunday to the Sunday after Easter. The 1983 Code extended the time for the Easter communion to Pentecost. In the United States, the time for the fulfillment of the Easter duty was extended by the Second Plenary Council of Baltimore (1830), probably due to the lack of clergy in some places. The "Easter season" for this purpose extended from the First Sunday of Lent to Trinity Sunday.

52. How is the Eucharist reserved during the Triduum?

B efore the beginning of the Triduum, the tabernacle is to be entirely empty; that is, all consecrated bread from previous liturgies has been consumed.

After communion during the Mass of the Lord's Supper, the consecrated bread which remains and that which has been prepared for communion on Good Friday is placed in a ciborium or similar covered vessel. Any consecrated wine is consumed.

A procession is formed and the Blessed Sacrament is carried to the place of reservation.

> For the reservation of the Blessed Sacrament, a place should be prepared and adorned in such a way as to be conducive to prayer and meditation; the seriousness appropriate to the liturgy of these days is enjoined so that all abuses are avoided or suppressed.
>
> When the tabernacle is located in a chapel separated from the central part of the church, it is appropriate to prepare the place of repose and adoration there
> (*Circular Letter* 49).

The "abuses" referred to in the *Circular Letter* may be the excessive use of candles, flowers, or other decorations which would distract attention from the tabernacle.

53. How does adoration of the Eucharist take place?

The Blessed Sacrament should be reserved in a closed tabernacle or pyx. Under no circumstances may it be exposed in a monstrance.

The place where the tabernacle or pyx is situated must not be made to resemble a tomb, and the expression "tomb" is to be avoided. The chapel of repose is not prepared so as to represent the "Lord's burial" but for the custody of the eucharistic bread that will be distributed in Communion on Good Friday.

After the Mass of the Lord's Supper the faithful should be encouraged to spend a suitable period of time during the night in the church in adoration before the Blessed Sacrament which has been solemnly reserved. Where appropriate, this prolonged eucharistic adoration may be accompanied by the reading of some part of the Gospel of St. John (chapters 13–17).

From midnight onwards, however, the adoration should be made without external solemnity, because the day of the Lord's passion has begun (*Circular Letter* 55–56).

Some parishes have the custom of adoration through the night. The *Circular Letter* does not forbid private prayer and reflection but restrains communal prayer, psalmody, or Scripture reading to the hours before midnight. This instruction simply reiterates the tradition and asks that the festive eucharistic celebration give way to the paschal fast.

54. What is meant by "Tenebrae"?

The word *tenebrae* means darkness. It was the name given to the pre-dawn service (Matins or Vigil) of Holy Thursday and Good Friday. One of the rituals performed during this service was the gradual extinguishing of all but one of fifteen candles placed in a triangular candelabrum in front of the altar and of all the lights of the church as morning broke.

This liturgy was sometimes anticipated in parish churches on Wednesday evening of Holy Week or, before the restoration of the Triduum, on Holy Thursday evening. The darkening of the church was thus all the more impressive, although the sense of the celebration had changed from welcoming the dawn to facing the night.

The *Circular Letter* advises a return to this practice while using the revised liturgy:

> It is recommended that there be a communal celebration of the Office of Readings and Morning Prayer on Good Friday and Holy Saturday. It is fitting that the bishop should celebrate the Office in the cathedral, with as far as possible the participation of the clergy and people.
>
> This Office, formerly called "Tenebrae," held a special place in the devotion of the faithful as they meditated upon the passion, death and burial of the Lord, while awaiting the announcement of the resurrection (40).

The Liturgy of the Hours describes how the two services may be joined together:

> Invitatory and Psalm 95
> Opening Hymn
> Psalmody of the Office of Readings
> Scripture Reading and responsory
> Patristic Reading and responsory
> Psalmody of Morning Prayer
> Reading and responsory

Canticle of Zechariah with its antiphon
Intercessions
The Lord's Prayer
Concluding Prayer
Blessing and Dismissal

This rather lengthy service may need to be adapted for parish use. The fundamental elements of the Hours, namely psalmody, Scripture, and intercessions, need to be respected. The current liturgy does not specify any ritual elements except the procession of the ministers and the incensation of the altar.

The use of other symbols such as candles or the placing of icons should also be in keeping with the overall spirit of the days and be in harmony with the parish's environment for worship.

55. Is it advisable to have the stations of the cross on Good Friday?

The *Constitution on the Sacred Liturgy* has this to say about all devotional practices:

> [D]evotions should be so fashioned that they harmonize with the liturgical seasons, accord with the sacred liturgy, are in some way derived from it, and lead the people to it, since, in fact, the liturgy by its very nature far surpasses any of them (13).

In this spirit, the *Circular Letter* makes this comment on other devotions on Good Friday:

> Devotions such as the Way of the Cross, processions of the passion, and commemorations of the sorrows of the Blessed Virgin Mary are not, for pastoral reasons, to be neglected. The texts and songs used, however, should be adapted to the spirit of the Liturgy of this day. Such devotions should be assigned to a time of day that makes it quite clear that the Liturgical celebration by its very nature far surpasses them in importance (72).

A well-celebrated Morning Prayer and the full celebration of the Lord's Passion in the afternoon or early afternoon may well satisfy the parishioners' need to go to church on Good Friday. In general, as with most liturgical decisions, where the custom has been well-established and does not conflict or interfere with the overall thrust of the day, let it continue.

56. What is the current thinking on proclaiming the Passion "in parts?"

The passion narrative contains a number of verses which are the response of the chief priests or of the crowd, demanding the crucifixion of the Lord. Some people object to the assignment of these words to the assembly, as though the assembly acts the part of unbelievers. The Roman tradition simply recognizes three readers:

> The passion narrative occupies a special place. It should be sung or read in the traditional way, that is, by three persons who take the parts of Christ, the narrator and the people. The passion is proclaimed by deacons or priests, or by lay readers. In the latter case, the part of Christ should be reserved to the priest.
> For the spiritual good of the faithful the passion should be proclaimed in its entirety, and the readings which precede it should not be omitted (*Circular Letter* 33).

Remember that the Passion is a proclamation of one of the central passages of the Gospel. It is not a script to be read through by actors.

Because of the length of the Passion Gospel, some variation in voices, sung responses, or pauses for silence will be helpful. Consider dividing the entire text into sections (as most editions of the Bible do) and assigning each reader one or two sections.

57. Must there be a homily on Good Friday?

The sacramentary states that "a brief homily may be given." The principal preaching moments are at the Mass of the Lord's Supper and during the Easter Vigil. The homily on Good Friday may be a brief introduction to a time of reflection and prayer or a simple and carefully worded highlighting of one message from the Scriptures that is most applicable to the assembly gathered there.

58. Should we use a cross or a crucifix for the veneration of the cross?

The origin of this rite is the veneration of the relics of the wood of the cross preserved in Jerusalem. The diary of Egeria (late fourth century AD) contains this description:

> The bishop's chair is placed on Golgotha Behind the Cross (the cross there now), and he takes his seat. A table is placed before him with a cloth on it, the deacons stand round, and there is brought to him a gold and silver box containing the holy Wood of the Cross. It is opened, and the Wood of the Cross and the Title are taken out and placed on the table.
>
> As long as the holy Wood is on the table, the bishop sits with his hands resting on either end of it and holds it down, and the deacons round him keep watch over it. They guard it like this because what happens now is that all the people, catechumens as well as faithful, come up one by one to the table. They stoop down over it, kiss the Wood, and move on. But on one occasion (I don't know when) one of them bit off a piece of the holy Wood and stole it away, and for this reason the deacons stand round and keep watch in case anyone dares to do the same again.

The veneration is paid to the fragment of the cross itself, not to an image of Christ. Note also the description of the current rite:

> For veneration of the cross, let a cross be used that is of appropriate size and beauty, and let one of the forms for this rite as found in the Roman Missal be followed. The rite should be carried out with the splendor worthy of the mystery of our salvation: both the invitation pronounced at the unveiling of the cross, and the people's response should be made in song, and a period of respectful silence is to be observed after each act of veneration—the celebrant standing and holding the raised cross.

The cross is to be presented to each of the faithful individually for their adoration since the personal adoration of the cross is a most important feature in this celebration; only when necessitated by the large numbers of faithful present should the rite of veneration be made simultaneously by all present (*Circular Letter* 68–69).

While a crucifix is perhaps customary, the liturgy clearly speaks of a cross "of appropriate size and beauty." Side by side with John's Gospel, the veneration of the cross is one of the triumphal moments of the Triduum, in which the cross is acknowledged as the tree of life, the ark of salvation, the sign of healing and reconciliation.

59. *Why is there no sign of peace during the Good Friday liturgy?*

The sign of peace was originally part of the preparation of the assembly for communion. Good Friday was originally an "aliturgical" day; that is, the Eucharist was not celebrated. Because there was no communion, there was no sign of peace. By the middle ages, the sign of peace as we know it fell out of common use except during Solemn High Mass; at such liturgies it was exchanged only among the clergy at the altar.

Communion for the faithful on Good Friday was added with the reforms of Pius XII (1951). The sign of peace was still not yet restored and so was not included in the rite. As will be explained further in question 60, the communion rite on Good Friday is kept to a minimum, in keeping with the spirit of the paschal fast.

60. Why is communion only under the form of bread on Good Friday?

The liturgy of Good Friday was formerly called the "Mass of the Presanctified," meaning that the eucharistic bread had been consecrated at a previous Mass. This is not as unusual as it may seem at first.

The eucharistic tradition of the church has two deep roots: 1) holy communion is the climax of the offering of the eucharistic sacrifice; 2) holy communion is the "daily bread" of the people of God. Ancient witnesses refer to the custom of people taking sizable portions of the consecrated bread home from the Sunday Eucharist in order to partake of the Body of Christ during the week or share it with family members. Monastic communities and rural churches without a resident priest might also partake of the presanctified Eucharist. This tradition appears in our own time in the various liturgical instructions which recognize both communion as the ideal participation in the Mass and as the daily spiritual food of the faithful which may be given apart from Mass, particularly to the sick. In all these instances, communion is under the form of bread; the consecrated wine is not reserved. The exception to the rule is that the Blood of Christ may be taken to the sick who are unable to partake of the host.

Part of this custom is practical: The reservation of consecrated wine risks both spillage and spoilage, whereas consecrated hosts are not difficult to preserve. Part of the practice is theological: Those who receive one species receive the Body and Blood of Christ, nothing more or less than those who receive both. And part of the custom is likely historical: Communion from the cup was in general disuse from the middle ages until after Vatican II.

Yet another point to consider is that the liturgy of Good Friday is in the midst of the paschal fast. Communion on this day is appropriately in the form of a fast-day meal, not a festive banquet.

---

61. *What do we do with the Blessed Sacrament after the Good Friday liturgy?*

A s with every eucharistic celebration, there should be nothing left over except for communion to the sick or, on Holy Saturday, to the dying. If possible, only the few necessary hosts may be placed in a pyx and the rest of the eucharistic bread consumed.

> When Communion has been distributed, the pyx is taken
> to a place prepared for it outside of the church
> (*Circular Letter* 70).

Usually this means a receptacle such as a safe in the sacristy. If there is no other appropriate place, the tabernacle of the church may be used. Any temporary place of eucharistic reservation may be dismantled after the church building is closed for the night.

62. Where is the cross placed after the Good Friday liturgy?

The Good Friday liturgy lacks a formal conclusion and invites by its silence a time of meditation:

> After the celebration, the altar is stripped; the cross remains however, with four candles. An appropriate place (for example, the chapel of repose used for reservation of the Eucharist on Maundy Thursday) can be prepared within the church, and there the Lord's cross is placed so that the faithful may venerate and kiss it, and spend some time in meditation (*Circular Letter* 71).

Ideally the church remains open but empty, except for the cross, throughout the day on Holy Saturday so that the people may do what the sacramentary describes: "On Holy Saturday the Church waits at the Lord's tomb, meditating on his suffering and death. The altar is left bare, and the sacrifice of the Mass is not celebrated."

---

63. *Our pastor says that it is now forbidden to hear confessions on Holy Saturday. Why is this so?*

The first rubric for Good Friday reads: "According to the Church's ancient tradition, the sacraments are not celebrated today or tomorrow." This was interpreted by some as meaning that the sacrament of penance could not be celebrated on Holy Saturday, contrary to the custom in many places.

Because "the sacraments" (literally, "the mysteries") in ancient usage meant "the Eucharist," this rubric was later interpreted as not referring to penance or anointing of the sick:

> On this day the Church abstains strictly from the celebration of the sacrifice of the Mass. Holy Communion may only be given in the form of Viaticum. The celebration of marriages is forbidden, as also the celebration of other sacraments, except those of Penance and the Anointing of the Sick (*Circular Letter* 75).

The ideal situation would be that all the faithful would be reconciled before the Triduum:

> It is fitting that the lenten season be concluded, both for the individual Christian as well as for the whole Christian community, with a penitential celebration, so that they may be helped to prepare to celebrate more fully the paschal mystery.

These celebrations, however, should take place before the Easter Triduum and should not immediately precede the evening Mass of the Lord's Supper (*Circular Letter* 37).

64. *Why is there Evening Prayer on Holy Saturday but not on Holy Thursday and Good Friday?*

The Easter Vigil is designed as an all-night liturgy, not an evening service. The expectation is that the Mass of the Lord's Supper will take place at the usual time of Evening Prayer and the celebration of the Lord's passion will likewise last until early evening. Because there are no early evening celebrations on Holy Saturday, Evening Prayer is said on this day.

65. How early may the Easter Vigil begin?

This question is the enduring legacy of the time when the Vigil took place on Holy Saturday morning. For most Catholics and other Western Christians, "Easter" means Easter Sunday morning, after sunrise.

The restoration of the Triduum by Pius XII envisioned the eucharistic liturgy of the paschal Vigil as commencing at midnight. This is the age-old practice of the Orthodox churches, still observed today. While Catholics accept (or even expect) a midnight service on Christmas, the association of midnight with Easter has been lost. Before long, concessions were granted which allowed the liturgy to take place in the evening of Holy Saturday, but after nightfall. Despite these regulations, some parishes begin the Vigil at the same time as the Mass of the Lord's Supper and the Liturgy of the Lord's Passion; some even revert to the usual time for Saturday evening Mass.

> The entire celebration of the Easter Vigil takes place at night. It should not begin before nightfall; it should end before daybreak on Sunday. This rule is to be taken according to its strictest sense. Reprehensible are those abuses and practices which have crept into many places in violation of this ruling, whereby the Easter Vigil is celebrated at the time of day that it is customary to celebrate anticipated Sunday Masses.
>
> Those reasons which have been advanced in some quarters for the anticipation of the Easter Vigil, such as lack of public order, are not put forward in connection with Christmas night, nor other gatherings of various kinds (*Circular Letter* 78).

We might also recall the Jewish tradition by which the Sabbath does not end until three stars are seen on Saturday night. The Easter Vigil should not begin until the Great Sabbath of Holy Saturday has passed. But for those who must follow a clock, it is sufficient to say that the entire Vigil must take place neither in the evening nor in twilight, but in the dark, generally understood as beginning about sixty to ninety minutes after sunset.

66. Any suggestions for the Easter fire?

In so far as possible, a suitable place should be prepared outside the church for the blessing of the new fire, whose flames should be such that they genuinely dispel the darkness and light up the night" (*Circular Letter* 82).

A "fire that illuminates the night" requires some careful preparation: a safe place, appropriate fuel, and permission from local authorities and the fire marshal. In the springtime, many areas experience rather volatile weather conditions. Unpredictable wind can make a large fire dangerous. But what can be more attractive and festive than a large fire on a damp, cold night? The whole bonfire experience may unnerve parishioners who will break into giggles with references to campfires and barbecues. Such is our disconnection with our ritual tradition. While we can manage bonfires for football games and Halloween, we seem to lose our expertise for the Triduum. Parishes may consider recruiting their local scout troop for this task.

Because of the work involved, many are content with a small brazier inside the church, without realizing the potential of smoke damage and irritation. An inside fire is best fueled by alcohol (isopropanol) and salt. This fire, however, is extremely hot and requires an unbreakable vessel.

87

67. Must we buy a new paschal candle every year?

This is probably a question which never occurred to our ancestors in the faith or to people who live in less technological, consumer-oriented societies. Only the invention of electric lamps and candle-shaped cylinders for various fuels makes this a point of discussion.

> The paschal candle should be prepared, which for effective symbolism must be made of wax, never be artificial, be renewed each year, be only one in number, and be of sufficiently large size, so that it may evoke the truth that Christ is the light of the world (*Circular Letter* 82).

Good liturgy demands authentic symbols; good ritual requires beautiful materials; festivity always involves some extravagance. Better a more striking (and likely more expensive) Easter candle than another row of lilies which will barely survive the octave. The Easter candle is *the* Catholic Easter symbol. It deserves to be magnificent.

If finances are tight or the parish simply wishes to consume less, the candle need not be wasted the following year. Many candle suppliers will accept the unused portions of previous Easter candles and credit the parish for the wax.

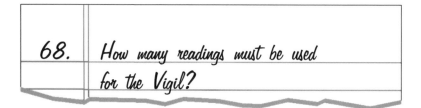

68. *How many readings must be used for the Vigil?*

This is a common but unfortunate question based on a misunderstanding of what a "vigil" is and the persistent approach to liturgy in terms of "the minimum required." There must be at least three Old Testament readings, including Exodus 14, and the epistle and Gospel.

The Easter Vigil was described by St. Augustine as the "mother of all vigils," that is, the preeminent example and pattern of Christian vigil-keeping. To vigil is to stay awake, to keep watch. For Christians, the vigil is a time to "wait in joyful hope" for the coming again of the Lord Jesus. The hours of the night-watch are punctuated by times of communal and individual prayer, especially prayer on the Scriptures. In 2 Peter 1:19 the prophetic message of the Bible is compared to a lamp upon which we fix our gaze while awaiting its fulfillment.

From this ancient tradition of prayer through the night focused on the Scriptures come the liturgical orders of vigil. One example is found in the Liturgy of the Hours: on Sundays and solemnities a service consisting of several psalms, canticles, and readings is proposed, climaxing in the reading of the Gospel of the resurrection or of the feast.

The "mother of all vigils" is that of Easter. Its "fundamental element" is "the reading of the word of God" (sacramentary, Easter Vigil, 21). In other words, the last element to be set aside should be the readings. The Easter Vigil Liturgy of the Word is designed to have nine readings, seven responsorial psalms and an extended alleluia verse: more than three times more than the typical Sunday liturgy.

While "pastoral reasons" may suggest reducing the number of readings, these reasons should be carefully considered and reviewed from time to time. Perhaps fewer readings and a more leisurely pace has helped our parish to participate more fully in the Vigil; it may now be the time to take another step toward its full celebration. Perhaps the seven Old Testament readings could be divided into a two-year cycle: readings 1, 3, 5, and 7 one year, readings 2, 3, 4, and 6 the next. Eventually, however, the parish should be using all the readings.

The liturgy requires at least three Old Testament readings with their psalms and prayers, and the epistle, alleluia, and Gospel. This minimum requirement should never set the standard.

69. May we use other songs in place of the responsorial psalm?

The psalms hold a privileged place in the liturgy because they are the prayers and songs inspired by the Holy Spirit. The responsorial psalms place the word of God in the mouths of the assembly so that they might fittingly respond to the word proclaimed.

As scriptural texts, the responsorial psalms should never be replaced by anything less than a metrical setting of the psalm or at least a hymn whose lyrics are thoroughly based on the psalms. No other hymns, no matter how popular or inspiring, are as worthy to serve as responses to the word.

The responsorial psalms at the Easter Vigil are a good example of how the liturgy itself helps us interpret the psalms. Even though the same text may be used on other occasions, the fact that *this* verse of *this* psalm is sung *at the Easter Vigil* invites us to understand that psalm as an expression of the paschal mystery.

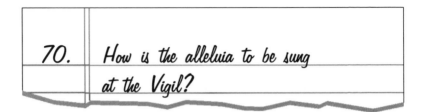

70. *How is the alleluia to be sung at the Vigil?*

The liturgical books describe a single alleluia, intoned by the presider and repeated by the assembly; this alleluia is repeated three times, each time on a higher pitch. This alleluia is, of course, the traditional and somewhat embellished Gregorian Chant setting. For communities unused to the simple elegance of chant, this alleluia may not adequately serve as the joyful acclamation of the resurrection Gospel. The alleluia of the Vigil is not a rite unto itself but the processional song for the Gospel, as on other Sundays.

The lectionary calls for a triple alleluia to be repeated between verses of Psalm 118. This extended Gospel acclamation provides a good opportunity for parishes to have (or introduce) a full procession of the Gospel, ideally through the assembly, accompanied by incense and other appropriate processional elements such as banners or hand-bells. Remember that candles are explicitly excluded from this procession at the Vigil.

As with the Easter Proclamation or Exsultet, the alleluia of the Easter Vigil deserves to be intoned by the best singer in the assembly.

71. What do the Elect do on Holy Saturday?

According to ancient tradition, they were to fast and bathe in preparation for their baptism. The *Rite of Christian Initiation of Adults* contains directions for this day:

> The elect are to be advised that on Holy Saturday they should refrain from their usual activities, spend their time in prayer and reflection, and, as far as they can, observe a fast.
>
> When it is possible to bring the elect together on Holy Saturday for reflection and prayer, some or all of the following rites may be celebrated as an immediate preparation for the sacraments: the presentation of the Lord's Prayer, if it has been deferred, the "return" or recitation of the Creed, the ephphetha rite, and the choosing of a baptismal name (RCIA 185).

The first directive should include the sponsors, godparents, cate-chists, and other liturgical ministers; ideally, the entire community participates in this Sabbath of reflection and fasting.

> Nevertheless, let the paschal fast be kept sacred. Let it be celebrated everywhere on Good Friday and, where possible, prolonged throughout Holy Saturday, as a way of coming to the joys of the Sunday of the resurrection may be attained with uplifted and welcoming heart (*Constitution on the Sacred Liturgy* 110).

72. *What about those who are not being baptized this year?*

They should take part as catechumens do in every liturgy: participate in the Liturgy of the Word at each Triduum liturgy and then be dismissed. Catechumens should, however, participate in the veneration of the cross on Good Friday.

73. We have never baptized anyone by immersion before. How can we introduce this option?

First of all, let's talk about what "immersion" is. The Roman rite provides for two forms of baptism: immersion and infusion (pouring). In some places, immersion is taken to mean the pouring of a large quantity of water over the whole body of the catechumen, who stands or kneels in a shallow basin. This author maintains that this is simply a generous infusion: water is being poured.

Immersion is the dipping or "submersion" of the body into a large container of water. The question of whether this was "the original form" of baptism is irrelevant. The Roman liturgy simply states that whether the water is brought to the catechumen or the catechumen is brought into the water, it is acceptable.

The logical next question is: Why bother? If pouring or immersing are equally valid, why immerse?

Immersion into water is threatening. It feels like drowning. Most of the Elect will instinctively grasp the side of the container (or the minister) when being lowered into the water. This natural reaction—fear—is part of the symbolism. Immersion signifies the death of the Lord, into which we have been led by the preaching of the Gospel. We are out of control; we have placed everything on the line.

Immersion into water is also refreshing. It feels like a warm bath after a hard day's work or a dip in the pool on a hot summer day. This experience of relaxation and cleansing is another part of the symbolism: liberation and new life. Our ambivalent experience with water has become the traditional sign of our entrance into the paschal mystery. We love it and we fear it; we risk and are renewed.

This human experience is amplified by all the scriptural stories of encounters with water: chaos and creation, Noah's ark, Jonah's fish, Jacob's well, Ezekiel's healing river, Jesus at the Jordan, the paralyzed man at Bethesda, the disciples on the Sea of Galilee, Paul and the women of Philippi, the crystal river of the new Jerusalem. These images should be brought to the faithful and the catechumens again and again until they actually start *asking for* immersion.

All that is required for actual immersion is a large enough container for water. Other issues will need to be addressed; the filling (and draining) of the container, heating the water, making sure that those coming out of the water will not slip on a wet floor, and designating places for changing clothes all need to be carefully planned. The container itself should be appropriate for use as a baptismal font. If a tub or pool is used, the exterior should be covered or enclosed.

The minister of baptism should practice the rite before the Vigil (and not with the Elect!) so that he is comfortable with assisting someone in and out of the water and can conduct the rite with appropriate grace and dignity during the liturgy itself.

74. *How do we baptize some, receive others, and renew the baptismal promises of everyone in the same service? When should the sprinkling rite take place?*

The blessing of the font is ancient; the renewal of baptismal promises is modern. The renewal of baptism gave us some way to retain the baptismal character of the Easter Vigil when the catechumenate had fallen into disuse.

When the Elect are present, their baptism is the primary focus of the rite. After they have been baptized (and are changing clothes) the members of the assembly, including the candidates for reception into full communion, are invited to renew their own baptism and may be sprinkled or invited to come to the font. After the water ritual is complete, the candidates make their profession and are received. Then the neophytes and candidates are confirmed. Note that the order in the *Rite of Christian Initiation of Adults* (appendix I, 4) supersedes the description in the sacramentary.

In spite of the ritual provision for this multi-layered initiation, the Easter Vigil is probably not the best time to receive other Christians into the full communion of the Catholic Church. Even though the Eucharist is the climax of the rite, it is the baptismal rite which tends to become the focus of the Vigil. The candidates are often confused with the neophytes, thus failing to respect their status as baptized Christians (see question 75).

75. Should the candidates wear baptismal robes?

This topic is not addressed by the liturgical rites themselves. Because everyone in the assembly renews his or her baptism, it does not seem appropriate to distinguish those who are being received from the rest of the faithful. The wearing of baptismal robes by the candidates may only blur the distinction between the Elect and the candidates.

Another way to approach this question is to ask whether baptismal robes are worn by those being confirmed or receiving their first communion apart from the Easter Vigil liturgy. If they do not, neither should the candidates. Remember, the candidates are not joining the church. They are being received into the full communion of the Catholic Church, but they have been members of the church since their baptism.

To use a different example, it is rare that married couples wear their wedding attire for an anniversary celebration. Some ritual garments are meant for a single occasion.

76. Isn't confirmation only administered by the bishop?

The administration of the sacrament of confirmation is one of the ways that bishops in the Western church retain their role of presider at the sacraments of initiation. Since at least the third century, priests and deacons have baptized, but the bishop "sealed" the baptism at another time, usually years later. This served to separate the two sacraments in the Western church and probably led to the understanding of confirmation as a ritual of maturity. (In the Eastern Church, the priest anoints the newly baptized with the *myron* or chrism consecrated by the bishop, thus making the bishop symbolically present at the baptism. The Roman Catholic Church considers all Eastern Christians "confirmed" at baptism.) In the early 1900s, Pope Pius X encouraged children to receive holy communion once they understood the meaning of the sacrament. Confirmation was not required for communion. Thus the sequence of baptism-Eucharist-confirmation, while not uncommon in various places, became the established norm throughout the Western church.

After Vatican II, the ancient sequence of baptism-confirmation-Eucharist was restored in the adult rite. The unity of the sacraments and the ancient sequence are considered more important than the rank of the minister. The rite and the *Code of Canon Law* expect that adults and children seven years of age or older will be confirmed during the same liturgy in which they are baptized or make their profession of Catholic faith. The priest who baptizes or receives the profession of faith is the proper minister of confirmation.

77.	*After all the other ceremonies of the Vigil, the prayer of the faithful seems redundant. Can it be omitted?*

On the contrary, the prayer of the faithful is even more important on this night. It is the neophyte's first sharing in the priestly prayer of the assembly of the faithful. This role is especially significant for those who have been dismissed Sunday after Sunday before the prayer of the faithful has been offered.

78. *We would like to make the catechumens'*
first communion more special.
What can we do?

O f course, this first sharing in the Eucharist is the climax of the
entire initiation process. It should be an unforgettable moment.
However, this does not mean cluttering the liturgy with additional
words or any kind of gimmick.

Let the ritual be itself: the breaking of the Bread of Life, the sharing
of the cup of salvation. Take a hard look at how the eucharistic ritual
is usually done on Sundays. Where is the awe, the reverence, the sense
of vitality, the dynamism of the community? Are the elements sub-
stantial? Are the vessels worthy? Are the actions graceful? Are the
elements handled with holy wonder? Is the approach to the altar by
the faithful truly a procession of those partaking in the wedding feast
of the Lamb? Do the ministers exude reverence for both the assembly
and the sacramental signs? Does the communion hymn radiate joy and
thanksgiving for the gift of being a eucharistic church? Celebrating
the Eucharist to the best of our ability is what will make everyone's
communion as unforgettable as their first.

When all this is done, perhaps consider a distinctive way to bring
the neophytes to the altar, for example, partaking of the Body and
Blood of the Lord at the table rather than at the usual communion
station, or have them approach accompanied by their godparents.
Work through the ritual elements and rehearse the ministers well.
Then let this gesture be reserved for the Eucharist of Easter night.

It is also appropriate for the presider to give the neophytes a brief
exhortation on the importance of the Eucharist just before the invitation, "Behold the Lamb of God" (RCIA 243).

79.	*The neighboring parish had a blessing of food after the Easter Vigil. What is the significance of that custom?*

The first meal of Easter breaks the paschal fast. The more rigorous the fast, the more significant this first meal became. Because our ancestors spent most of the Triduum in church, the preferred Easter foods were those that could be prepared in advance and served cold or with a minimum of cooking—for example, hams or sausages. It was also customary to include among the foods those items which had been forbidden for the entire lenten time, such as eggs and other dairy products. Special sweet breads decorated with crosses or other Christian symbols are also typical.

The blessing of Easter foods would serve as a fine beginning to the reception or celebration provided for the neophytes and newly received.

The rite found in the *Book of Blessings*, chapter 54, may be used either after the Easter Vigil or after the Mass on Easter Sunday morning.

80. When should we decorate the church for Easter?

Two approaches come to mind. Because the Vigil is the first celebration of the Great Sunday, all may be prepared in the early evening hours before the liturgy begins. This often becomes a morning event, thus filling the Great Sabbath with activity. Visitors to the church on Saturday afternoon will find it full of decorations and flowers and not the quiet empty place the liturgy describes. A pre-Vigil decoration session will require a fair amount of coordination and planning, lest we exhaust our volunteers before the Vigil begins.

Another option is to wait until the Vigil is finished and take some time after the liturgy for a communal decorating of the church. But this seems to suggest that Easter does not begin until Sunday morning.

The *Circular Letter* steers a middle course and calls for placing flowers at the altar during the singing of the Gloria during the Vigil liturgy itself. A well-rehearsed procession with candles and flowers would be striking ritual. One must ask, however, if this custom continues the former liturgy's separation between the "Vigil" and the "Mass of the Resurrection." The ritual books, it should be noted, conceive of decorations in simple, almost austere terms. The large floral displays some churches create for Easter are not envisioned in the rites.

One priest in this author's diocese served for some time as a chaplain in a community of religious women. He used to order corsages for all the sisters to wear, explaining that he simply wanted to decorate *the Church* for Easter.

Easter

81. What are the liturgical symbols of Easter?

The most important liturgical symbol is always the assembly of the faithful. During the Easter season the neophytes (newly baptized) hold first place among us. It is in the neophytes that we recognize the Lord Jesus risen from the dead. In ancient times, the neophytes wore their white baptismal garments to church for the entire Easter octave.

The second most important liturgical symbol is the Easter candle. This candle remains in the sanctuary, near the ambo or a similar prominent place, and is lighted for every liturgical service through Pentecost. Ideally the candle is large enough that it might remain burning between Masses, at least on Sundays, so that its witness to the resurrection is not diminished.

A third characteristic of the Easter season is the singing of alleluia. Outside of Lent, the alleluia fittingly accompanies the proclamation of the Gospel, in which the risen Christ speaks to us each day. But during Easter, alleluia is added to every antiphon of the liturgy and should rightly be included in every hymn.

The font, in which the water blessed during the Easter Vigil remains throughout the Easter season, deserves attention as well. The parish's baptismal font should be a significant container, and the presence of water in it should be remarkable enough. Unfortunately, this is rarely the case. Special tanks are often set up and decorated for the Vigil, only to disappear with the lilies. Another unfortunate practice is the creation of elaborate fountains which have nothing to do with baptism or even the renewal of baptism. A permanent fountain is surely a welcome feature of the courtyard, garden, or gathering space; it does not belong in the sanctuary or baptistery unless it is part of the font and its waters are blessed and used in sacramental celebration.

In addition, white vestments and flowers at the altar are a familiar sign of festivity. Parishes may wish to have a set of white vestments that is worn every day of the Easter season—and exclusively during that time.

Some "symbols" are foreign to the Roman liturgy. A large wooden cross draped with a white cloth does not signify Easter in our tradition. There is more to the resurrection than an empty cross or tomb.

Similarly, statues of the risen Christ are questionable. Resurrection is, after all, not the same as resuscitation. An image of Jesus loosely draped in a shroud and portraying his mortal features contradicts the Gospels, which describe him as unrecognized by his disciples. (Not to mention that the shroud was left in the tomb!) The transcendence and power of the resurrection is beyond our comprehension; it should certainly not be limited by a soulless representation.

If the church usually displays a crucifix above the altar, this is not contrary to the Easter mystery, for it is the resurrection of the Crucified One that we proclaim. The image on the cross reminds us of the historical reality; our breaking of the bread enables us to touch the mystery.

82. **How is the Easter season presented in the lectionary?**

The lectionary during the Easter season, especially on weekdays, provides us with semi-continuous readings of the Acts of the Apostles and the Gospel of John. "Semi-continuous" means that each book is read in its own order (though some chapters or sections may be omitted). There is no attempt to harmonize or match the first reading to the Gospel.

The Acts of the Apostles traces the development of the early church from a small company of disciples to a network of communities spread throughout the Roman world. Acts recounts some momentous events: the gift of the Holy Spirit and the continuation of Jesus's ministry through the apostles, the conversion of Saul of Tarsus, the acceptance of the gentiles, the decision of the Jerusalem community that the Law of Moses was not a prerequisite for membership in the Christian church, and the missionary journeys of Paul.

The Gospel readings present those sections of John which were not read during Lent. The Gospels serve as mystagogia on baptism and Eucharist (Jn 3 and 6). The images of Christ as the good shepherd and the vine, the description of the role of the Holy Spirit, and the priestly prayer of Christ are among the passages read during the fifty days.

Note that, according to tradition, the Old Testament is not read during the Easter season, even on the feasts or memorials of saints or at ritual Masses (confirmations, weddings, ordinations, funerals). The Acts of the Apostles or the Book of Revelation are read in place of the Old Testament historical or prophetic books. This reflects the understanding that the Easter season, the Great Sunday, is the beginning of the new creation; what we celebrate during Eastertime is the fulfillment, not the promise or foreshadowing.

As during Holy Week, it is important not to interpret passages referring to the first-century relationship between church and synagogue as justification for anti-Semitism.

83. What is the purpose of the Sequence on Easter Sunday morning?

The liturgical hymns known as "sequences" are poetic and musical elaborations on the alleluia verse in the previous Roman liturgy. The sequence serves as an extended introduction to the Gospel procession and reading.

The current liturgy requires the sequence on Easter and Pentecost. Sequences on the Solemnity of the Body and Blood of Christ ("Corpus Christi") and the memorial of Our Lady of Sorrows (September 15) are optional. A fifth sequence, *Dies Irae*, which formerly associated with the funeral liturgy, is now placed in an appendix to the Liturgy of the Hours for optional use on All Souls Day.

Because the sequence is a hymn, it is best sung. If the resources of the particular assembly do not allow for this to be done well, it is permissible to recite the poem. When recited, the poetic text is always preferred.

84. Should we renew baptismal promises again on Easter Sunday?

The renewal of baptismal promises on Easter Sunday morning is an adaptation approved for the dioceses of the United States. This seems to ritualize the fact that many more people attend Easter Sunday Masses than attend the Easter Vigil. It seems odd that we should renew our baptismal promises at the Easter Vigil, only to do it again within a few hours.

The renewal of baptismal promises is the secondary element of the baptismal liturgy (see question 74). If the parish community assembles in large numbers for the Vigil and essentially the same community is present again on Sunday morning, perhaps one or other renewal should be chosen. In this example, if baptism is celebrated at the Vigil, perhaps the renewal should be kept for Sunday morning.

85. What is the octave of Easter?

The first eight days of the Easter season are a week-long extension of Easter Sunday. For this reason they are named "Easter Monday," "Easter Tuesday," and so on. The days are ranked as solemnities. As on Sunday, the Gloria is part of each day's liturgy. Daily the alleluia verse proclaims, "This is the day the Lord has made, let us rejoice and be glad," and the liturgy concludes with the double alleluia.

The first readings, from Acts of the Apostles, begin the semi-continuous reading of that book (see question 82). The Gospels, however, are the various post-resurrection appearances of Christ from each of the four Gospels. In this way, each day is a new proclamation of the Lord's resurrection.

The Liturgy of the Hours repeats the antiphons and psalms of Easter Sunday on each day of the octave, again emphasizing the "today" of the Easter mystery throughout the week.

In addition, Easter Preface I and the special inserts for Eucharistic Prayer I are used throughout the octave.

86. *What about funerals and weddings during the octave of Easter?*

The order of funerals including the funeral Mass may be celebrated during the octave of Easter, except on Sundays. The first and second readings are not taken from the Old Testament but from Acts of the Apostles or Revelation.

The wedding Mass (and other ritual Masses for that matter) may not be celebrated during the octave. The rite of marriage may be used, but the readings and Mass prayers are of the day.

87. *Our parish never uses the sprinkling rite except during Easter time. Why is this?*

The blessing and sprinkling of water on every Sunday was ordered by the ninth-century Pope Leo IV. Since the middle ages this rite was a preparatory service just before the principal parish Mass. Today the sprinkling rite may substitute for the penitential rite on any Sunday of the year. This rite helps to emphasize Sunday as the day of resurrection; by replacing the penitential rite it adds a certain festivity to the Sunday Eucharist. The themes of baptismal renewal and the Lord's Day are found within the prayers:

> Dear friends, this water will be used
> *to remind us of our baptism....*
> God our Father, your gift of water...washes away our sins
> and brings us eternal life.
> We ask you now to bless this water,
> and to give us your protection *on this day*
> *which you have made your own.*
> Renew the living spring of your life within us...
> (emphasis added).

Because Eastertime, as the Great Sunday, is a special time for the sacraments of initiation, the blessing and sprinkling of water as a reminder of our baptism is especially suitable during this season. Some parishes may use the sprinkling rite every Sunday during Easter to remove any penitential elements from the liturgy.

The sprinkling rite is not restricted to the fifty days of Easter. A special Easter season blessing prayer is provided in the sacramentary.

88. *The fifty days of Easter just seem lost among all the other activities. How can we emphasize them?*

To the extent that Sunday has been lost as a day of festivity, it will be difficult to make much sense of the "Great Sunday," the fifty days of Easter.

Visually, the worship environment (both inside and outside) should proclaim the Easter mystery consistently for fifty days. In most places, the traditional Easter lilies will last about two weeks. The decorating committee should plan ahead for replacement flowers for every week until Pentecost. (This may mean restraint on the flower budget for Easter Sunday.) Where spring flowers have arrived during this time, the external environment may need only a few banners or similar decorations to highlight the Easter decorations provided by the Creator (with the help of the parish garden club!).

If the parish has "fasted" from meetings and other business activities, Eastertime may feel like a return to business-as-usual before the summer vacation season sets in. If business meetings are necessary during the Easter season, some festive element should be included: singing during the opening prayer, reading from the Easter lectionary or from other authors about our new life in the paschal mystery, extra time for refreshments and fellowship.

EASTER

89. How are the saints commemorated during the Easter season?

During the weekdays of the Easter season, except during the octave, the memorials and feasts of the saints are celebrated as at other times during the year. If an apostle or martyr is commemorated, red vestments are worn. On memorials it is preferable to use the readings of the day and sing the alleluia so as to maintain the ongoing Easter story and spirit. Votive Masses should not be celebrated except for significant pastoral cause.

90. What were the Rogation Days and Ember Days?

Rogation Days are days of solemn prayer usually associated with blessing of fields and seeds during the spring. The Roman Calendar before Vatican II provided for four rogation days: one on the feast of St. Mark (April 25) and the others on the Monday, Tuesday, and Wednesday preceding the Ascension.

The Ember Days were the Wednesday, Friday, and Saturday following the Third Sunday of Advent, the First Sunday of Lent, Pentecost Sunday, and the Feast of the Holy Cross. Ember Days were days of fasting and vigil as well as days for celebrating the sacrament of holy orders. Ember Days ceased to be days of fast and abstinence with the 1966 reform of penitential observances.

The 1969 reform of the liturgical calendar notes that dioceses may designate annual days of solemn prayer for various needs.

91. Why does our music director refuse to play hymns to the Blessed Mother during May?

Most of us have grown quite comfortable with overlapping cal-endars. The civil year runs January to December. The school year runs from September to June. The liturgical year begins on the First Sunday of Advent and hinges on the two major cycles of Advent-Christmas-Epiphany and Lent-Easter-Pentecost. Meanwhile a popular devotional calendar grew up among Catholics in which months of the civil year were assigned to particular devotions: May is the month of Mary, June the month of the Sacred Heart, October the month of the rosary, November the month of the faithful departed.

The month of May generally corresponds to the last half of the Easter season. The continued popularity of May devotions is due to the important role of Mary in Catholic devotional life as well as to the tendency for the Easter season to fade from our minds. Thus, unfortunately, "May" becomes more important than "Easter."

It is also important to note that the primary place of music in the liturgy is the singing by the people of acclamations and responses (responsorial psalm; alleluia; Holy, holy, holy, among others), and the singing of prayer texts such as the preface. In past practice, however, singing tended to be concentrated on hymns placed at various "pauses" in the liturgical actions: entrance, offertory, communion, recessional. The hymns most often chosen in the past were those known from vernacular devotional services such as novenas or Bene-diction.

The parish music director is simply holding to the principle that devotional hymns are usually inadequate to accompany the liturgical action of the assembly. A hymn honoring Mary does not adequately accompany the procession of the people to communion, for example.

The Roman liturgy only provides Marian liturgical texts on Marian feasts, unlike some Eastern liturgies which have incorporated various hymns and antiphons to the Mother of God into the regular eucharistic celebration. There are a few texts which are specifically Eastertime antiphons or hymns honoring Mary. For example, the *Regina caeli laetare* ("Queen of heaven, rejoice") is used at the conclusion of Night Prayer.

If local custom dictates some recognition of Mary at Mass during May, a Marian recessional hymn is a possibility because this final hymn is not strictly a part of the Roman eucharistic liturgy.

92. What is the May Crowning devotion?

The practice of depicting the Blessed Virgin Mary enthroned and/or wearing a regal crown began in the fifth century, at the time of the Council of Ephesus. There is a liturgical rite for the "crowning" of an image of the Blessed Virgin Mary derived from the practice of embellishing or ornamenting already existing icons or statues for reasons of devotion or thanksgiving. This rite is celebrated for the crowning of an image which is the object of pilgrimage and similar public expressions of faith and is therefore reserved to the bishop or his delegate.

Regarding the parish custom of a "May Crowning," the Bishops' Committee on the Liturgy writes:

> The crowning of such images may be the object of a devotional service which takes its inspiration from the various texts and rites of the *Order of Crowning an Image of the Blessed Virgin Mary*. "May crownings" and other laudable pious practices expressing devotion to the Mother of God which are in keeping with the norms of Pope Paul VI's Apostolic Exhortation *Marialis Cultus* may indeed be led by priests, deacons, and lay persons (Newsletter [Oct. 1986]).

If the devotion of the parish recommends a "May Crowning" celebration at a weekday Mass, the presider may use a votive Mass of the Blessed Virgin Mary (for example, the Mass prayers and preface from the *Collection of Masses of the Blessed Virgin Mary*, no. 29, *Mary, Queen of All Creation*) even on a weekday of the Easter season. The placing of a crown or wreath of flowers on the parish's image of the Virgin Mary might best be done during the entrance song of the Mass or after communion. Otherwise the crowning should take place at Evening Prayer or a Liturgy of the Word.

Devotion to the Mother of God retains a significant place in Catholic spirituality. Past excesses have been maligned as the "deification" of the Virgin. Some zealous people have wrongly contrasted the sweet and gracious Mother with the angry, punishing Son. Today's liturgical texts seek to present an image of Mary entirely in accord with the Scriptures: as virgin, mother, disciple, woman of faith and prayer, model of the church, and participant in the paschal mystery of Christ her Son. All Marian devotion should lead the faithful to a renewal of their baptismal promises and a more authentic discipleship of Jesus.

93. What's wrong with preaching about Mother's Day?

The real issue here is the nature of a liturgical homily. It was only a generation ago that Catholics listened to sermons during Sunday Mass. This author recalls how the priest would read the Scriptures in Latin at the altar, then go to the pulpit, read the Epistle and Gospel once more in English, read the various announcements for the week, announce the topic or Scripture verse on which the sermon was based, make the sign of the cross, and preach the sermon. When this was done, the sign of the cross was made once more and the priest returned to the altar to resume the liturgy. The sermon thus functioned as a separate "service" sandwiched between the two halves of the Mass.

Paragraph 24 of the introduction to the reformed lectionary describes the integral role of the homily in the liturgy:

> Through the course of the liturgical year the homily sets forth the mysteries of faith and the standards of the Christian life on the basis of the sacred text....The purpose of the homily at Mass is that the spoken word of God and the liturgy of the eucharist may together become "a proclamation of God's wonderful works in the history of salvation, the mystery of Christ" (see *Constitution on the Sacred Liturgy* 35, 2). Through the readings and homily Christ's paschal mystery is proclaimed; through the sacrifice of the Mass it becomes present (see CSL 6, 47). Moreover Christ himself is also always present and active in the preaching of his Church (see Paul VI, encyclical, *Mysterium fidei*, 3 Sept 1965; *Ad gentes* 9; *Evangelii nuntiandi* 43).
>
> Whether the homily explains the biblical word of God proclaimed in the readings or some other texts of the liturgy (see CSL 35, 2; *General Instruction of the Roman Missal* 41), it must always lead the community of the faithful to celebrate the eucharist wholeheartedly, "so that they may hold fast in their lives to what they have grasped by their faith" (CSL 10)....But

this demands that the homily be truly the fruit of meditation, carefully prepared, neither too long nor too short, and suited to all those present, even children and the uneducated (see John Paul II, apostolic exhortation *Catechesi tradendae* 48).

Thus the homily is not an element which stands alone but must be integrally related to the scriptural readings which precede it and the sacramental celebration which follows.

If this is true of the homily, it is also true of the liturgy. The celebration of the mystery of faith does not exist in a vacuum. The liturgy is always "today," celebrated by these people, in this time, in this cultural context. Although secular observances cannot replace the paschal mystery (especially during the Easter season), we also cannot pretend that they do not exist.

Mother's Day is a secular observance, originally organized as a protest movement on behalf of peace. The *Book of Blessings* notes that this observance:

> has an important place in American life. Since it occurs on the second Sunday of May, during the Easter season, the Mass of the Sunday is always celebrated. However, in order to provide some recognition of this holiday, model intercessions and a prayer over the people are provided... (1724).

The key is "to provide some recognition." It may well happen that the meaning of the Easter Scriptures is illuminated by examples from family life, particularly the role of the mother. It is certainly appropriate to pray for the mothers of the parish and to bless them. The secular holiday cannot, however, become the entire theme of the liturgy.

One final note: In these days when a "traditional" family structure cannot be assumed, care should be taken that the honoring of mothers does not exclude other women who exemplify other dimensions of motherhood within the community: adoptive mothers, godmothers, grandmothers, and all who nurture our children.

---

94. What ever happened to Ascension Thursday?

The mystery of the ascension (or return of Christ to God the Father) is expressed in each of the Gospels in different ways. In Matthew, the ascension occurs with the commissioning of the disciples on a designated mountain in Galilee. No interval of time is specified. One of the endings of Mark's Gospel describes the ascension as taking place at the end of a meal with the disciples. Again, the Gospel merely says that this happened "later." Luke's ascension story takes place in Bethany, late in the evening of "the first day of the week," after the meal at Emmaus and the apparition to the Eleven. John's Gospel has Jesus ascending just after his encounter with Mary Magdalene early on Easter Sunday morning; however, Jesus appears three times to the disciples after this "ascension."

The story of the ascension as told in Acts 1 is the origin of the forty-day separation between Easter and Ascension Day. This exact counting of forty days places the Ascension on Thursday of the sixth week of Easter.

The 1969 reform of the calendar notes that wherever the Ascension is not celebrated as a holy day of obligation, it is transferred to the Seventh Sunday of Easter, which becomes its proper day in the calendar (*General Norms for the Liturgical Year and the Calendar* 7). The 1983 *Code of Canon Law* gave the conferences of bishops the authority to decide which of the ten universal holy days of obligation would be observed in their regions. At the time of this writing, the Ascension has been transferred to the Seventh Sunday of Easter in Canada and several western states.

95. Isn't the Easter candle supposed to be put away after the Ascension?

The Easter candle as a sign of the risen Christ remains in its place of honor, either near the ambo or in another place in the sanctuary, throughout the fifty days. Only after Evening Prayer II of Pentecost is the Easter candle removed to the baptistery. It remains there so that the candles of the newly baptized may be lighted from it.

The Easter candle is taken from the baptistery only to be placed near the body of the deceased. Apart from baptisms and funerals, the Easter candle is not lighted outside the Easter season.

96. *I heard of a parish that has a novena to the Holy Spirit. What is that?*

A novena is a nine-day period of prayer. Most novenas in the past were devotional services honoring the Blessed Virgin Mary or another saint. The custom of nine days may be traced to the gathering of the disciples between the ascension of the Lord and the coming of the Holy Spirit on Pentecost.

The parish custom referred to here is a commemoration of that original novena: people are gathering to pray for renewal in the outpouring of the Holy Spirit. The *Ceremonial of Bishops* notes: "The weekdays from Ascension to the Saturday before Pentecost inclusive are days of preparation for the coming of the Holy Spirit, the Paraclete" (376).

The traditional gifts (Isa 11:2) or fruits (Gal 5:22–23) of the Spirit provide appropriate focal points for prayer and reflection. Other possibilities would be a parish mission or retreat, evenings of reflection for various groups in the parish, a series of presentations on living the gifts of the Spirit, or further mystagogical catechesis on the Scriptures proclaimed during the Easter season.

However observed, the last days of the Easter season summon us to more fervent prayer as we anticipate a new Pentecost among us.

97. How can we celebrate the Vigil of Pentecost?

Encouragement should be given to the prolonged celebration of Mass in the form of a vigil, whose character is not baptismal as in the Easter Vigil, but is one of urgent prayer, after the example of the Apostles and disciples, who persevered together in prayer with Mary, the Mother of Jesus, as they awaited the Holy Spirit (*Circular Letter* 107).

One way to celebrate the Vigil of Pentecost is to celebrate the Eucharist and include all the Old Testament readings given in the lectionary. As at the Easter Vigil, each reading is followed by a responsorial psalm, a time of silent prayer, and a collect. The climax of this vigil is not sacramental initiation but "urgent prayer," a solemn and intensive litany of intercessions, as on Good Friday.

Another model is Evening Prayer joined to the Eucharist, as provided in the Liturgy of the Hours. Still another is the Office of Readings for Pentecost, extended by the use of the canticles and Gospel reading indicated in the Liturgy of the Hours.

The Vigil of Pentecost is also an excellent opportunity for ecumenical prayer. Since most Christian communities would celebrate the Eucharist or holy communion on Pentecost Day, the vigil (without Mass) allows many denominations to come together and share in prayer and reading of the Scriptures. We may well pray that this Pentecost will be the last time we must withhold the Eucharist from one another.

| 98. | *Shouldn't we renew our confirmation on Pentecost, just like we renewed our baptism at Easter?* |

The sacrament of confirmation finds its place in the rites of initiation. Due to historical circumstances emphasized by theologizing on the practice, confirmation has come to be a sacrament which stands alone.

Vatican II called for a revision of the rite so that the sending of the Spirit might be seen as a part of the paschal mystery. The 1972 revision of the rite attempts to ritualize a connection among baptism, confirmation, and Eucharist by providing that confirmation take place during Mass and include the renewal of baptismal promises.

Some attempt to understand the link between baptism and confirmation by referring to Easter and Pentecost: baptism is our participation in the death and resurrection of Jesus Christ; confirmation is our sharing in the descent of the Holy Spirit. The paschal mystery is one, even though celebrated on various days; so also our initiation into Christ is one mystery, ritualized in the sacraments. We are baptized and confirmed but once; our sharing in the Eucharist becomes our ongoing affirmation and exercise of our baptism.

The liturgy does not provide for a "confirmation renewal" because confirmation itself is a seal and renewal of baptism.

99. Why do some people call Pentecost "the birthday of the church"?

The mystery of church is intimately linked to the mystery of the Trinity, especially the sending forth of the Holy Spirit through Jesus Christ. In this way, the manifestation of the Holy Spirit on Pentecost (Acts 2) with the subsequent missioning of the apostles to preach to the nations may be considered the beginning or birth of the church. It is worth noting that other texts refer to Good Friday as the birth of the church "from the side of Christ as he slept the sleep of death upon the cross" (*Constitution on the Sacred Liturgy* 5). Similarly, the incarnation is also the beginning of the church.

The liturgy does not, however, use the term "birthday." Birthdays in our society are significant events, but a good deal of frivolity is associated with them. Pentecost is not about balloons and candles on a cake and gag gifts; these have no place in our liturgy. Pentecost is renewal, commencement, embarking upon adventure, enthusiasm, joy. Pentecost is not the anniversary of the incorporation of a great institution. Pentecost is how the disciples of Jesus discover what it means to live the Gospel.

100. Should other languages be used for the Pentecost Sequence?

The question of other languages is a delicate one. In multilingual communities it seems a natural way to include the prayer of the whole assembly, particularly on the day when the many languages of the world came together to profess one faith. However, the mystery of Pentecost is not limited to the variety of human language groups. Use of various languages unknown to the assembly may only mystify them and obscure the meaning of the feast. The question to be asked, as in all liturgy, is: Does this assist the assembly in their active participation, or is this being done only to "symbolize" something from history?

101. I understand that the Easter season concludes with Pentecost. How can we symbolize that?

The liturgical end of the Easter season is very simple: At the conclusion of Mass (and Evening Prayer) on Pentecost Sunday the double alleluia is sung, as during the octave of Easter. Afterward, the Easter candle is placed in the baptistery. It remains there so that the candles of the newly baptized may be lighted from it; it may also be placed near the body of the deceased during the funeral liturgy.

A better question may be how to symbolize that Pentecost is the fiftieth day of Easter, the completion of the "days of Pentecost." Some parishes dismantle (what remains of) their Easter season environment and try to create an entirely new look for Pentecost Sunday. This approach is a return to the time when Pentecost was its own feast: It had its own vigil, complete with the blessing of the font, and its own octave, concluding with Trinity Sunday.

If "Holy Spirit" banners must be used, why not put them in place from the day after the Ascension? If red flowers and other decorations are going to be used, be sure that they are coordinated with the entire Easter season environment.

In other words, we need to see the mystery of Pentecost as already present throughout the Easter season, indeed, through the entire liturgical year. The very beginning of creation recognized the breath of the Spirit. It was by the Spirit that the Virgin Mary conceived the Messiah, whose mission was confirmed by the apparition of the same Spirit above the Jordan River. The Spirit rejoiced in Jesus' ministry and was sent forth from the cross; it was finally bestowed in its fullness on the first Easter night. This mystery of the descent of the Holy Spirit is that by which the church lives and carries out its mission of evangelization and reconciliation. The festival of Pentecost marks the end of the Easter season as sunset brings every Sunday to a close, somewhat quietly and gently, for tomorrow we rise to return to our daily work. As Sunday and its Eucharist become the fount of power for our lives in Christ, so the fifty days of Easter refresh us in our mission to transform and sanctify our world.

Works Cited and Suggested

Adam, Adolph. *The Liturgical Year*. New York: Pueblo, 1981.

Bouyer, Louis. *Liturgical Piety*. Notre Dame: University Press, 1955.

Cantalamessa, Raniero. *Easter in the Early Church*. Collegeville, Minn.: Liturgical Press, 1993.

Congregation for Divine Worship. *Circular Letter Concerning the Preparation and Celebration of the Easter Feasts*, 1988.

Dallen, James. *The Reconciling Community*. New York: Pueblo, 1986.

Delaney, John J. *Dictionary of the Saints*. Garden City: Doubleday & Co., 1980.

Huck, Gabe. *The Three Days*. Rev. ed. Chicago: Liturgy Training Publications, 1992.

International Commission on English in the Liturgy. *Book of Blessings*. New York: Catholic Book Publishing Co., 1989.

———. *Ceremonial of Bishops*. Collegeville, Minn.: Liturgical Press, 1989.

———. *Documents on the Liturgy*. Collegeville, Minn.: Liturgical Press, 1982.

———. *General Instruction on the Liturgy of the Hours*. New York: Catholic Book Publishing Co., 1975.

———. *Sacramentary*. New York: Catholic Book Publishing Co., 1985.

The Liturgy Documents: A Parish Resource. 3rd ed. Edited by Elizabeth Hoffman. Chicago: Liturgy Training Publications, 1991.

Mitchell, Nathan, OSB. *Cult and Controversy: The Worship of the Eucharist Outside Mass*. New York: Pueblo, 1982.

Pawlikowski, John T., and James A. Wilde. *When Catholics Speak About Jews*. Chicago: Liturgy Training Publications, 1987.

Talley, Thomas. *The Origins of the Liturgical Year*. New York: Pueblo, 1986.

Weiser, Francis X. *Handbook of Christian Feasts and Customs*. New York: Harcourt, Brace and Company, 1952.

Index

abstinence 15, 16, 17, 117
alleluia 7, 21, 107, 110, 112, 116,
    118
    double 112, 131
    of the Vigil 89, 92
    triple 92
anamnesis 59
anointing of the sick 84
Ascension 3, 117, 125, 126, 131
    celebrated on Thursday 124
Ash Wednesday 3, 4, 5, 13, 15, 19,
    22
ashes 13, 25

baptism 4, 18, 19, 49, 52, 62,
    95–96, 97, 99, 125
    by immersion 95–96
    by infusion (pouring) 95
    celebrated during Lent 24, 29
    preparation for 18, 29, 43, 44,
        49, 52, 93
baptismal promises, renewal of 4,
    98, 111, 114, 121, 128
baptismal robes 98
benediction 26–27
Blessed Sacrament 82
    adoration of 72

exposition of 26
    reservation of 59, 71, 72, 82
blessing(s) 26
    of food 102
    of oils 38
    of palms 36
Book of Blessings viii, 102, 123
Book of the Elect 48

candidates 29, 45, 47, 48, 52, 97, 98
catechesis 4, 7, 19, 30, 43, 44, 47,
    126
catechumens 4, 43, 44–45, 46, 47,
    50, 53, 54, 94, 95, 96, 101
chapel of repose 71, 72, 83
Chrism Mass 38, 63
color(s), liturgical 35, 41
communion 70, 80
    during Triduum 40, 81, 84
    first 97, 98, 99
confirmation 24, 43, 97, 98, 99, 128
    administered by bishop only 99
convert/conversion 44, 47, 54
Council of Nicaea 9

Easter vii, 3, 6, 24, 29, 30, 41, 67,
    86, 89, 102, 103, 107–132
    candle 7, 88, 107, 125, 131

Easter (*continued*)
  communion 70
  determining date of 8–9
  duty 70
  fire 87
  octave of 3, 107, 112, 113, 131
  season 7, 70, 107, 109, 114,
    115, 116, 118, 120, 123, 125,
    126, 131
  Sequence 110
  symbols of 107–108
  Vigil 7, 22, 41, 54, 77, 85, 86,
    89–90, 91, 97, 100, 107, 111,
    127
Egeria 78
Ember Days 16, 117
environment *See* liturgical
  worship, environment for
Essenes 8
Eucharist vii, 26, 30, 40, 43, 46,
    66, 67–69, 80, 84, 97, 101,
    114, 128, 131
  adoration of 72
  benediction of 26–27
  exposition of 26
  institution of 59, 61, 62, 64
  reservation of 71, 82, 83
Evening Prayer 7, 57, 85, 120, 125,
    127, 131
exorcism 50–51, 52
Exsultet 68, 92

fasting 4, 5, 6, 13, 14, 15, 16, 17,
    19, 21, 25, 28, 31, 35, 43, 65,
    72, 80, 81, 93, 102, 117
feasts 32, 109, 116
  Marian 118
fifty days 3, 7, 109, 114, 115, 125,
    132
font 24, 25, 95–96, 97, 107, 131
footwashing 58, 59, 61, 62
forty days 4–5, 18, 124

funerals 125, 131
  during octave of Easter 113
  during Triduum 40
  on Holy Thursday morning 6

Gloria 21, 59, 103, 112
Good Friday 6, 15, 23, 40, 41, 65,
    66, 71, 72, 73, 75, 77, 80, 81,
    82, 83, 84, 85, 93, 94, 127,
    129
Great Sunday 7, 15, 103, 109, 114,
    115
Gregorian Calendar 9

Holy Saturday 4, 6, 15, 40, 41,
    53, 54, 65, 66, 73, 82, 83, 84,
    85, 86, 93
Holy Thursday 3, 6, 29, 38, 40, 66,
    73
holy water 24
Holy Week 3, 4, 24, 28, 32, 37, 65,
    73
hunger cloth 23

illumination 49

Julian Calendar 9

Laetare Sunday 19, 35
lectionary viii, 7, 18–20, 92, 109,
    122, 127
Lent vii, 13–54, 65, 84, 102, 107,
    109
Leo IV 114
liturgical documents viii
liturgical worship vii, ix, 26, 68
  environment for 21, 25, 74, 103,
    107–108, 115, 131
  formalism of ix
  trivialization of ix
liturgical year vii, 7, 60, 118, 122,
    131

Liturgy of the Hours 33–34, 41, 73, 89, 110, 112, 127

mandatum rite 58, 59, 61, 62
Mardi Gras (Carnival) 17
Mary 118–119, 131
  devotions to 120–121
Mass of the Lord's Supper 57, 59–60, 63, 64, 66, 71, 72, 77, 84, 85
Mass of the Presanctified 81
Maundy Thursday 58, 83
May Crowning 120–121
memorials 3, 32, 33, 109, 116
  optional 32
minister of initiation 50, 96, 99
Morning Prayer 33, 35, 73, 75
Mother's Day 122–123
mystagogy 109, 126
  as time of reflection 7

neophytes 97, 101, 102, 107
ninety days vii
novena(s) 126

oil of catechumens 38, 54
oil of the sick 38

Palm Sunday 3, 36, 37, 70
paschal candle 88
paschal mystery vii, 6, 18, 84, 95, 121, 122, 123, 128 See also Easter candle
Passion Sunday 29, 36, 37
Passiontide 23, 36
Passover 8, 67–69
  seder meal 67
penance 4, 13, 19, 49, 65
penance, sacrament of (confession) 70, 84
  options for services 30–31
penitential celebrations 30–31, 84

penitents 13, 21, 23, 31
Pentecost 3, 7, 70, 107, 117, 125, 126, 128, 131–132
  as birthday of the church 129
  Sequence 110, 130
  Vigil of 127
Pius X 99
Pius XII 6, 80, 86
presentation of the creed 43, 53
presentation of the Lord's Prayer 43, 53, 93
priestly service 38, 64
psalm(s) 33, 89, 91, 112, 118, 127
purification and enlightenment 4, 43, 44, 49, 54

quartodecimans 8
Quinquagesima 3

reconciliation 4, 21, 30, 79, 131
resurrection vii, 6, 7, 8–9, 18, 65, 67, 73, 93, 107–108, 112, 128
Rite of Christian Initiation of Adults 20, 43, 47, 49
rite of election (enrollment) 4, 29, 43, 44–45, 46, 47, 48
Rogation Days 117

sacramentary viii
saints' days 3, 32, 34, 35, 109, 116
scrutinies 4, 18, 29, 30, 43, 50, 52
Septuagesima 3
Sequence See Easter Sequence; Pentecost Sequence
Sexagesima 3
sign of peace 80
solemnities 3, 15, 16, 32, 89, 112
sprinkling rite 114
St. Augustine 89
stations of the cross 26–27, 75
submersion See baptism by immersion

Sunday 7, 131
    as feastday of the resurrection
        vii, 29, 114
    as preferred day for infant
        baptism 29
    never a day of fast 15
    never a day of penance 4

Te Deum 34
Tenebrae 73–74
transfiguration 18
Triduum vii, 6, 57–103
    communion during 40
    funerals during 40
    music during 42
    reservation of Eucharist during
        71
    weddings during 28

uncatechized adults 30
unleavened bread 67

veiling of statues and images 23, 36
veneration of the cross 23, 78–79,
    83, 94

washing of feet *See* footwashing
weddings
    during Lent 28
    during octave of Easter 113

More Resources for Liturgy

Modern Liturgy Answers
The 101 Most-Asked Questions about Liturgy
Nick Wagner

Paper, $14.95
144 pages, 5½" x 8½", 369-8

Everyone has a question about liturgy. Get answers from the editor of MODERN LITURGY magazine. You'll learn the historical and theological background of current liturgical practices — and you'll get practical solutions to vexing pastoral problems. Use this important reference book for your planning — or just to provide quick authoritative answers.

The Lent Book
An ML Book Edited by Lonni Collins Pratt

Paper, $29.95
176 pages, 8.5" x 11", 446-5

Now you can plan more creative Lenten liturgies with this important resource. It provides many commentaries, songs, and ideas for the Lenten season. Assembled by the editors of MODERN LITURGY, this collection of practical resources will help you plan worship services that are as powerful as possible. *The Lent Book* will serve as a fountainhead for your creativity and give you a wealth of ideas for your worship planning.

The Triduum Book
the Editors of Modern Liturgy

Paper, $24.95
192 pages, 8½" x 11", 394-9

Start your annual liturgical planning with the Triduum — and start your Triduum planning with *The Triduum Book*. Assembled by the editors of MODERN LITURGY, this collection of practical resources will help you celebrate the paschal mystery as powerfully as possible. *The Triduum Book* is an updated revision of the *Holy Week Book*. Make sure your parish has a copy.
